Heal
Negative
Energies

ANNE JONES

Healing Negative Energies

Published in the UK in 2002 by
Judy Piatkus (Publishers) Limited
5 Windmill Street
London W1T 2JA
e-mail: info@piatkus.co.uk

Reprinted 2003

A catalogue record for this book is available from the British Library

ISBN 0 7499 2366 0

Edited by Peter Bently
Illustrations by Rodney Paull

Typeset by Palimpsest Book Production Limited, Polmont, Stirlingshire
Printed and bound in Great Britain by The Bath Press, Bath, Somerset

Contents

	Acknowledgements	vii
	Introduction	1
1.	My Energy Experiences	5
2.	Overcoming Self-negativity	31
3.	Other People's Negativity	85
4.	Negative Energies in Food and Drink	131
5.	Negativity in Objects and Places	150
6.	Electromagnetic and Earth Energies	185
7.	Curses and Magic	220
8.	Spirit Presence	245
9.	Choose the Positive	271
	Postscript	281
	Further Reading	282
	Index	287

Dedication and Acknowledgements

This book is dedicated to my dog Prince – who taught me how strength of spirit and zest for life can overcome all fears and physical challenges. Thank you, dear Prince, for your unconditional love and absolute devotion.

I would like to thank Ginny Surtees, who has been the most inspiring and helpful editor. I would also like to thank Peter Bently for his inspired assistance and all the members of the Piatkus editing team who have helped me complete this book. I also thank my mother and Sophie for their support and peaceful presence while I toiled away at the computer.

I would also like to thank the following experts and therapists whose brains I have picked relentlessly. Alyce Holst for her help and support and information on electronic gem therapy. Janet Thompson for her past life regression therapies that have unlocked doors for me. Dr Louis Alicea, my brilliant chiropractor who has corrected the self-inflicted damage caused by too many hours on the computer. Mark Rendell for his help with Feng Shui practices and for a beautiful new garden where I can restore my peace and harmony. Dr David Webb and Henley-Gawler and Associates for their valuable insights into electromagnetic geopathic stresses. Sue Rogerson and Flora Azulay for sharing their knowledge of ionisers, products that protect us from phone and computer emissions, and Skenar and electromagnetic therapies.

Remember that the force of light is stronger than darkness. When we switch on a light the darkness will always, always disappear.

Introduction

I could feel the hairs on the back of my neck start to rise. Then I felt a creepy sensation move down my arms and back. What was going on? This was supposed to be a holiday retreat, a place of peace and tranquillity, a chance to step back in time to a world before technology and fast communication. Yet here I was, feeling anything but peaceful: in fact I was downright disturbed!

I had booked into a delightful hotel in the middle of the South African karoo desert. The hotel complex had been designed out of a small village, built in the 19th century around a railway station – a small post office, a school house, a couple of private houses and the railway station itself. The place was steeped in history and extremely fascinating and charming, but for me it proved to be very spooky.

I had been fine during the day, when there were lots of people around, either staying at the hotel or stopping for a meal on their way through to Cape Town in the south. But now it was bedtime and I had entered my room to unpack and settle down for the night. As soon as I closed the door and moved into the room I started to feel uncomfortable – the room seemed cold and slightly menacing. There was little I could do so I started to sing to distract myself – my singing is capable of distracting most people! Eventually I felt calmer and slipped into bed and due to the exhaustion of driving six hours that day I fell asleep.

That night I had a dream. I dreamt that I was in a room filled with men in uniform. They were all heavily bandaged and in terrible pain and despair. I could feel the suffering and misery that these soldiers were experiencing and I woke up shivering and cold. I picked up the guide book by my bed and started to read the history of the settlement. I soon found what had caused my distress. In the Boer War the hamlet had been used as a field hospital for the local troops!

What I had been experiencing in that hotel were the energies of the past – the pain and suffering of the soldiers had become imprinted on the buildings and I had felt and sensed this over a hundred years later. I have had many experiences similar to this throughout my life. This sensitivity to energies and atmospheres was rather a nuisance in my earlier years, as I felt the discomfort of others either living or long gone and I had no way of controlling the sensations. However over the years I have developed this awareness into a sensitivity to all energy, both positive and negative, and ten years ago I started natural energy healing. Since then I have learnt to clear and lift up people's personal energy and also that of their homes and workplaces.

In this book I share with you some of my experiences with many kinds of negative energy, including that caused by ourselves, the people around us, electrical equipment, misaligned earth energies, black magic and the presence of spirits. I will pass on the techniques I have learnt and developed to clear and protect against negative energies, to ensure that you are not only positive and uplifted yourself but that your surroundings are also light and free from negative influences.

Whatever the cause of negative energy – whether it comes from natural sources, or is created by humanity's thoughtlessness or by our own fears and anxieties – there are ways to counterbalance and minimise the effects. Humanity has managed to survive and adapt to many changes in the environment, from drastic climatic alterations to changing sources of food, and we have overcome a variety of challenges to our well-being, from plagues to physical oppression, where our livelihood, homes and families have been threatened.

Today, in addition to the old challenges, there are new ones such as electromagnetic stress and microwave emissions from mobile phones. I believe we are able to surmount these new challenges and bring ourselves into a positive, peaceful and harmonious state. We can do this by using the power of our minds, our determination to overcome any threat to our well-being and our intention to enjoy a happy and healthy existence. As we work on making ourselves positive and healthy, so the effects of this personal inner work and healing will eventually have a far-reaching and wider result. What we start in the home will eventually ripple through to our community, our country and the rest of the world.

I sincerely believe that we influence our environment by the way we are, the way we think and our attitudes. We will make a difference by taking a positive and upbeat attitude to our lives and by keeping our home and workplace clean and tidy and treating the environment with respect. We can replace the negativity and darkness in our world with positivity and light. If each and every one of us does our bit then before we know it the world will be a lighter and brighter place, and love and peace will prevail for the good of all.

In the first chapter I will tell you about my own spiritual 'education' and my first experiences as a healer. Later, we will look at clearing ourselves, our homes and our workplaces of all but the very lightest of energies. So are you ready for the greatest detox of your life? Let's go.

1

My Energy Experiences

In this chapter I will tell you how as a child I first became aware of the energy that exists both in and around us and how it can affect us both positively and negatively. Later, as a result of several significant experiences, I developed this awareness into something more – an ability to heal and to clear negative influences.

A Sensitive Child

I have always been sensitive to atmospheres. When I was a child I could tell immediately on entering a room if my parents were anxious, depressed or angry. Fortunately, they rarely argued, but when I was four my father lost his job in the civil service and he struggled to find a new position in the difficult times of post-war Britain. This put a heavy strain on both my parents. My father was a natural worrier and this also affected my mother and made her anxious too, so I sometimes came downstairs to see her in tears. At this time they lived in constant fear of the future as they saw their savings gradually depleted. I felt the stress and anxiety that they were experiencing as a palpable force that had entered our home.

Happily, my father finally found a job in personnel that was far better suited to his caring and sensitive nature than his civil service post of statistician. Immediately the atmosphere in the house changed, and as my parents became happier and more relaxed I could feel my own spirits lifting.

However, I also sensed that there was some tension and mystery around my relationship with my parents. Whenever forms had to be filled in for school, I felt them becoming tense. When I was twelve I wanted to go with the church Sunday school to Oberammergau in Bavaria to see the famous Passion play. Although the cost was the reason they gave for why I couldn't go, I suspected and sensed that it involved some underlying fear of theirs. I thought at the time that they feared for me travelling so far without them. I felt the same nervous energies when, at the age of fifteen, I was given the chance to go with the school to Spain. I would have needed a passport, and this seemed to be the nub of the problem. I could feel fear and anxiety from both my parents despite their attempts to cover up their emotions.

By the time they finally sat me down to talk about it I was convinced they were going to tell me I had been adopted. In fact I wasn't entirely wrong. It transpired that my real father had left just after I was born and 'Dad' was in fact my stepfather. But he and my mother had been unable to marry because his wife was still alive and refused to give him a divorce. So my parents had lived with the secret that they were not married and that I was not my stepfather's daughter. When I wanted to go abroad they would have had to fill in passport forms that revealed the truth of their relationship, and this was the cause of those tense moments.

With today's more enlightened approach to marriage and partnerships this may seem strange, but in those days there was real disapproval of people living together and my parents had mainly wanted to protect me from gossip. But what they had in fact done was create tension and fear, which of course I had sensed.

Once I realised that the father who had brought me up with so much love and care was not even related I just burst into tears. What love and kindness he had given to me, and I wasn't even his daughter. This was not the reaction they had expected, so there was incredible relief all around. They had thought that I would be devastated to find out about my father and had dreaded telling me the truth. Imagine carrying the burden of their secret all those years and without any real cause.

At that time and for many years after I was unaware that it was other people's emotions that I was picking up. Often if I sensed these energies I would get butterflies in my stomach and think that I was 'nervous' for some reason. Later on in my teenage years I had a problem going to parties or joining any large group, because I would be overwhelmed by these nervous feelings as soon as I entered the room. It was annoying, as I loved meeting people, but often it was really uncomfortable. I realise now that I was picking up the energies of the group, or of one or two individuals in the group who were upset in some way.

You may also find that some of the feelings and anxieties you experience are not your own – you may in fact be sensitive to the energies that other people are emitting into the surrounding atmosphere. Next time you go to a party or gathering, take note of how you feel. Are you nervous, on edge or apprehensive before you leave your home or when you join the group?

When people are angry, nervous or fearful the energy of their emotions and thoughts will send out negative vibrations into their surroundings. If they are happy, joyful and having fun they will emit positive vibrations of energy. These vibrations are the 'vibes' that you pick up when you enter a room and mix with others. Later in this book I will be showing you ways in which you can protect yourself from the negative emotions, and even thoughts, of other people.

A spirit presence in our home

Apart from being aware of other people's emotions, I have also been sensitive to 'spiritual' or 'otherworldly' energies. For as long as I can remember I have lived with ghosts. Not that I call them ghosts now – 'spirits' is the correct description for the apparitions and beings that sometimes share our homes and whose presence can be felt and sensed – and occasionally seen – by the privileged few. I say 'privileged' because I feel that my encounters with the spirit world have been remarkable, uplifting and, in some cases, quite entertaining experiences.

In more recent years, the ability to sense the presence of the unseen has stood me in good stead in my work as a healer. I have found my sensitivity to different energies and their beneficial or detrimental effects on people a great asset but, as is often the case, the learning process wasn't all fun and at times it was downright scary.

My very earliest exposure to souls that linger around

after death occurred in our family home in Putney in south London, where I lived in a Victorian terraced house with my mother and father from the age of two until I was twenty. Even before I was five I can remember waking in the night and hearing odd noises. It sounded to me as though someone was walking up and down in the room above me, and – I know it sounds like an absurd cliché – I could hear what seemed like the dragging of chains.

Night after night I would lie awake, fascinated by these noises and imagining what was making them. I wasn't too frightened, as at that age I had no knowledge or fear of ghostly, spiritual or psychic phenomena. I asked my mother what the noises could be and she hastily concocted a story about the neighbours cleaning their grate. I was not convinced – who cleans their grate at two o'clock in the morning? – and just put my mother's reasoning down to her lack of understanding.

Years later I confronted my mother with her feeble explanation and she admitted that she knew of the haunting but hadn't wanted to frighten me. As a result I grew up thinking that all houses had visitors in the night who dragged around a bundle of chains. Fortunately, most of the time the sounds stayed upstairs, but one night I heard steps on the stairs leading down to my room and when the bedroom door handle rattled I must admit that I became very, very nervous! I lay totally still and eventually I sensed whatever it was moving away. I then ran as fast as I could to the comfort and security of my parents' bedroom.

When I was a teenager my mother also had a visitation from our unearthly houseguest. She was taking an afternoon nap when her bed started to shake and her pet dog, who was resting in the room with her, jumped up and started to run around the room in a frenzy of barking.

Of course, no one was physically there but my mother was aware of a presence and recognised that she had been visited by a spirit of some kind. We discussed the situation and as we talked I sensed that the spirit must have been the old lady who had been the previous owner of the house. She had bequeathed it to her daughter, who was now our tenant. But the will had been destroyed and the other family members had sold the house to my parents, sharing the proceeds.

We had bought the house with the daughter in occupation as a sitting tenant. Not only was the daughter extremely upset and angry at not owning the house herself – she was not the friendliest of tenants as a result – but obviously her mother was also so distressed and attached to the situation that she was still earthbound and hadn't moved on to lighter realms. In most instances of the 'haunting' there was nothing to fear and we were just troubled by the disturbed mind and emotions of a sad old lady.

When I was older I learnt how to assist souls who have been so affected by upsetting experiences that they cannot bring themselves to leave their earthly home. Later in this book I will show you how to help souls to move on and hopefully I can take away some of the mystique and fear associated with what are in fact quite natural and harmless occurrences.

Becoming a Healer

My natural sensitivity to the presence of spirits in houses and negative atmospheres didn't develop into a healing skill until I moved to Malaysia with my husband in 1992. My introduction to our new life there got off to a rather bad start. My husband had been to see the company-owned house that was to be our home and came back with a rather lacklustre report. 'I don't think you're going to like it,' he announced. 'It's very dark.' That was all the description I could get out of him – 'It's very dark'. He went on to tell me it had a swimming pool and that perked me up somewhat, and he also told me that that it was surrounded by tropical growth – despite the fact that this was in a suburb of a modern city.

I soon found out what he meant by dark. On my arrival I stepped into the dark and gloomy front hall then into the living rooms which were also extremely depressing and murky. My heart sank. The house wasn't actually that old – it had been built in the 1950s – but on three sides it was surrounded by large tropical trees and shrubs that stopped natural light coming through the windows. I was immediately overcome by a heaviness of heart and despair. The entire house smelt dank and mouldy and despite the fact that the previous tenants had only just left it also seemed neglected and unloved. I felt so depressed that I sat down and cried. Even as I sat there in my misery I felt the presence of many spirits. I would later discover that we had twenty-two spirits in the basement.

I've never been down for long and soon cheered up when I realised that I was being very ungrateful. Here I was in a new country with great opportunities ahead. I was about to enjoy a privileged lifestyle with an in-house cook, cleaner, driver and all the joys of expatriate living. I soon realised that I could make a difference to the mood of the house myself. I asked the spirits in the house to leave me alone and not to disturb me in any way. Then I changed everything that it was in my control to change. I selected the colours and the contents of the house and put my own personal stamp on the property.

I lifted up the energies of the house by decorating and furnishing it with light and bright colours and fabrics. I had a wonderful time shopping and choosing things for the home that would offset its gloomy nature. I put pictures on the walls and new rugs on the black marble floors, filled the hall with flowers and lamps and it soon started to feel like a warm and inviting home. I also found that having people around for dinner and parties helped to lift the energy of the place and it began to feel much happier and lighter. So if you also have a house that seems dark and uninviting do whatever you can, whatever is within your control, to brighten it. Your intentions and endeavours alone will make a difference to the energy of the place. You will be amazed what you can do with the right colour paint and a few plants and flowers.

Spiritual awakening – the call to start healing

Malaysia was in fact going to be my spiritual and metaphysical school and university all rolled into one. While I lived in that house I experienced my true spiritual awakening one day when I heard a voice telling me to start healing. This was like a shot out of the blue. Suddenly I was facing a complete change of my life. I was told who to approach to help me get started – one of my fellow-expatriate colleagues. I quickly contacted her and, to my surprise, she had been expecting me for some time.

In her meditation she had received a message that she should help me with my first steps to becoming a hands-on healer. I took to it quite naturally and spent all my spare time practising on friends and family. My sensitivity to energy now came into its own and I began to use my hands to feel and shift the negativity that blocks the natural flow of life-giving energy around the body.

Spirit guides: our unseen helpers

I discovered that we all have constant help and supervision in our lives from those who have passed on into the spirit world. These unseen helpers guide us through our lives even though we are often unaware of their assistance. The messages and warnings that they send us come through as intuitive thoughts and feelings.

Have you ever had the feeling that you should not go somewhere or take a certain route, without understanding why – you just know that you shouldn't? Very often these unheard messages are coming from your spiritual guides, who are often family members who have passed on. For example, my 'wake-up' call came from my grandmother, who died before I was born.

I started to meditate regularly and soon discovered I had other guides, who taught me a simple process of intuitive healing and gave me symbols that activate healing energies. With these symbols and the process of clearing and energising I can help people remove the blocks of old emotional experiences and raise the level of their energy so that they can be revitalised and healed, mentally, physically and spiritually.

This form of healing has been called 'spiritual healing' or 'hands-on healing' in the past but I think 'natural energy healing' is a better description of the process. In this book I will describe how to do it and show you some of the symbols so that you can clear the negativity of everyday life from yourself, your family and friends.

The gift of 'seeing'

As I started to practise my new-found healing skills I realised that I had acquired the ability to 'see' with my mind's eye. When I focus on someone in order to heal them, I can visualise things in my mind that relate to their problems. Sometimes I see an incident from a past life, sometimes an experience from earlier in this life. These help me to understand the root cause of my client's problem.

Eventually this gift of 'seeing' developed, allowing me to connect to the spirit world and not only to sense the presence of spirits but also to see 'ghosts' and lost spirits as though I was watching mini video clips in my head.

The role of distance healing

I learnt another useful skill at this time, one that is easy for anyone to use. This is 'distance healing'. As we are entirely made of energy, every thought we have takes emotions and energy to the person we are thinking about. You can use this fact to send love and healing to your loved ones, wherever they are. By focusing on a person and visualising them as well and surrounded by light you can actually help to improve their health and well-being.

I started to do this regularly and I have had some amazingly successful results. I have since shown hundreds of people how to do it and we now have an established distance healing group through the Hearts and Hands organisation. If you want healing or want to assist in sending healing to those in need please contact us through the website www.heartshands.org.

Helping Lost Spirits – What I Learned in Egypt

While I was living in Malaysia I also learnt to help move 'ghosts' or 'stuck spirits' on to the higher realms of existence – where we should naturally go when we die. A friend of mine called Morna and I took a trip from Kuala Lumpur to Egypt. There I had a bizarre but enlightening experience in Tutankhamun's tomb that led me to develop new healing skills.

It was my first trip to Egypt and Morna and I had joined a group of seventy in Cairo. We had arrived earlier than the rest of the group and had already tasted the exotic and mystical energies of Egypt during a ride around the pyramids at Giza. I found the energies of the sacred sites very powerful, despite the number of tourists everywhere, and I was itching to see the really wonderful temples and ancient tombs situated along the Nile.

We joined a cruise ship at Luxor that was to take us up the Nile to Aswan. Included was a visit to the Valley of the Kings, one of the highlights of the trip, to explore tombs of the ancient pharaohs and see the wonderful wall paintings in these monuments to the kings of the past.

During my morning meditation I asked my spiritual guides if there was anything I should consider in the day ahead. I was amazed and delighted to receive a direct and clear message that I should examine the west wall of Tutankhamun's tomb and there I would find a message that I would find relevant to my life's work. I was absolutely beside myself with excitement and couldn't wait to get there. You may well know something of the story of Tutankhamun's tomb, but here is a short summary for those of you who have not heard it before.

In the 1920s Lord Carnarvon led a team of archaeologists under Howard Carter into an area of the Western Desert near Luxor where many tombs of the pharaohs of ancient Egypt had already been uncovered – it was to become known as the Valley of the Kings. It was the custom in ancient Egypt to assist the spirit of the departed pharaoh on its journey through the underworld by burying with the body its most precious possessions. Carnarvon's expedition discovered the well-hidden entrance to a tomb that had not been opened by earlier explorers or archaeologists and was virtually untouched by the tomb robbers of the past. This was unprecedented. Thieves had already plundered virtually every royal tomb that had been found in the previous century. So it was a momentous occasion when Carter and his team broke through into the small but largely untouched tomb of the young boy king Tutankhamun.

The sarcophagus still held the mummified body and it was surrounded by the most amazing treasures of gold, precious gems and other stunning artefacts. They removed all the artefacts and some of these are now on show in the Cairo Museum (which is a must to visit). However, they also discovered by the entrance of the tomb a dire warning – a curse would fall upon anyone who touched or removed the ancient treasures.

Over a relatively short period of time the curse seemed to take its toll as a number of the original team died, mostly suddenly and unexpectedly. Lord Carnarvon himself died in his hotel in Cairo and, at the same time at his home, Highclere Castle near Newbury in England, his pet dog lifted up his head, howled and also passed away. Our tour guide, Achmed, told us that, fortunately, the curse doesn't apply to visitors who want to just go and take a look.

My visit to Tutankhamun's tomb

You can imagine it was with much excitement that I set off on the journey to the Valley of the Kings. We left our cruise ship and took a *felucca* – a local sailboat – across to the other side of the Nile, where we were met by a coach that took us deep into the desert. On the way Achmed told us there were only three tombs open to the public that day – one of which was Tutankhamun's. He also said that due to the interest in that particular tomb and because it was so small, the authorities wanted to dissuade people from entering so there would be an extra levy to pay. I paid up without a moment's hesitation. Hopefully there would be fewer visitors and I would be able to investigate this west wall message in peace.

I left the rest of our group and went over to the tomb's entrance. I must say I felt a chill as I went inside, thinking of the curse. I quickly ran down the passageway leading to the heart of the tomb where Tutankhamun's body lay in its massive sarcophagus (Carter had the king's body autopsied and then returned it to the tomb). I looked around and there were drawings from *The Book of the Dead* – the ancient Egyptian guide to the land of the dead – on three walls surrounding the body. Now I had a problem – which was the west wall? A member of our group had joined me so I asked him if he had any way of knowing which direction was west and, as it happened, he reached into his pocket and pulled out a compass.

I peered up at the west wall and there was a painting of the solar boat which, in Egyptian mythology, takes the soul of the departed on its journey to the underworld. Sitting on either side of the soul – depicted by a scarab – sit two apes. These are the guardians of the soul and they are holding out their hands and healing the soul. It took me a second or two to consider what this message meant for me. I then realised that this was to be my new work – to heal the souls of the departed.

When we die our soul leaves the body and moves on to other levels of consciousness, of existence. These levels are called the 'astral planes' and this is where we stay until it is time for us to return to Earth for our next incarnation. So my new work was to help souls once they have died and help them ascend to the light of the astral planes – to Heaven. I felt a great 'whoosh' come over me – a sure sign that I had correctly understood the message.

The Valley of the Artisans – a painful experience

After the Valley of the Kings we moved on to visit the Valley of the Artisans. This is where the workers who constructed the great tombs of the kings were buried. These tombs are much smaller and not nearly so magnificent as their masters', but are interesting nevertheless. I queued up to enter the steep shaft that led down to one of the two tombs open for visitors. Suddenly Morna rushed up out of the tomb holding her head. 'It's terrible down there, it's given me a dreadful headache.' She really did look ghastly. However, I was determined to go down and see for myself. As I stepped off the staircase that led down to the lower levels I also felt a pain in my head. I felt too a prickling all over me and as well something I would come across many times in the future – the sensation that I was covered in cobwebs. It was also very, very cold there – in sharp contrast to the heat of the desert above.

I realised that I was alone apart for one other member of our group. I closed my eyes and then I 'saw' in my mind's eye a scene that related to the headache. A group of men were chasing a single man across the desert and they were hitting him continuously over the head with sticks. Eventually he fell down and they continued to hit him until he died. The disturbed and negative energy of the tomb and the associated pain in the head were coming from the presence of his spirit.

With eyes still closed, I intuitively spoke to him and told him that he was dead and needed to move on. I asked him to look up and see the light of the higher realms and to move towards it. I saw him doing this and floating off to be consumed in the light. I opened my eyes and then shared my experience with my travelling companion. Amazingly, she also said that she had been aware of a presence and she confirmed that it had now left. The atmosphere had become lighter and felt warmer than before and I realised then what an impact these lost souls can make on our environment as they hang on to their earthly existence.

So that was the beginning of a 'career' move that has taken me to many places where there are spirits that need assistance to move on to the light. It is beautiful work and very rewarding, because the clearing has not only helped to make homes easier to live in but it has also helped the departing soul move to its rightful place.

Over the years I have learnt to do this away from the actual location and I often find it an easier method, since I am not distracted by the anxiety of working in a haunted building. The distance process is a far less threatening experience for beginners in this field, as you will see when I describe my technique to you in Chapter 8. I personally love doing this work and hope that you may join me in it.

Learning How to Lift Curses and Black Magic

Another skill I acquired in Malaysia was to manage the effects of black magic. Despite the sophistication of modern Malaysia, black magic is still practised. I met a judge there who told me that many of the country's leaders and businessmen are victims of curses and spells sent by *bomo*s, the local healers or witchdoctors, employed by their rivals and competitors. I have to say that I think she was exaggerating, but there are people in every society who are unscrupulous enough to use any power they can to further their positions. The old crafts and practices of the shamans are still around in Malaysia, and this knowledge is sometimes used by people to further their own ends. However, I doubt if the average person living in one of the cities gives black magic a second thought, or even knows how to find a *bomo*.

My housekeeper, Saro, presented me with my first experience of lifting a curse. One day she called me in some distress and told me that her husband had been cursed. I admit I found it hard to accept this, coming from a Western society where cursing is something of a rarity these days. Anyway, I said I would meet him and see if there was anything that I could do to help.

He hobbled towards me. One leg was incredibly swollen and causing him great pain. He said that he had no knowledge of harming himself in any way and that he had woken up with his leg in this state. I noticed that although as an Indian his skin was brown, the leg that was causing him pain was almost black. He was a large, well-developed man who normally enjoyed good health and was a regular visitor to the gym. He told me that one of his colleagues wanted his job and had been to a *bomo* to put a curse on him so that he was unable to work.

This was my first healing session where a curse was the source of an illness, but I was to see many such cases over the next few years. I wasn't absolutely sure what to do at that time so I just swept away the negativity and channelled in healing energy to raise his total vibration. I could feel dark and sticky energy around his leg and the now familiar 'cobwebby' feeling that I associate with heavy and turgid negative energy. I also felt the hairs on my neck stand up, which I now recognise is a sign of black magic or mystical work. I can't say that I was particularly successful on that occasion but Saro's husband said he felt better after my treatment. In the event he decided to visit the *bomo* himself and told me later that this man had actually pulled out needles from his leg – after which he recovered very quickly.

Discovering Energy Imprints

I discovered that objects can hold strong energies when I was in my twenties on a business trip to Ankara in Turkey. During my stay I met members of an American film crew who were kicking their heels around the hotel while waiting for their equipment to be released from customs. One evening I met them in the bar and they were showing off their purchases from the local market. One of the crew had something quite special, a silver necklace with a small, beautifully carved container which held a small roll of paper. It seemed that this was a prayer and could have been a memento from a Haj, the Muslim pilgrimage to Mecca.

The necklace was passed around the group and each person who took it went quiet and quickly passed it on. It came to me and I felt myself go cold as I held it. It caused me to feel goosepimples and sent shivers down my spine and I quickly gave it back to the young American who had bought it. He looked at my face and asked me what was wrong. I told him it felt as if it had really negative 'vibes' and I was sure something quite bad had happened to its previous owner. Since then I have learnt that an article can absorb emotions or thoughts of the owner as the thoughts are a form of energy and they will merge with the energy of the object. If the original owner of the necklace had had a bad experience which involved fear, then the negative energies of the fear could well have passed into the necklace itself.

I didn't see the group again but one evening a week after I returned home I was having dinner with a friend when I suddenly experienced the same goosebumps and shivers. I felt as if part of me was being dragged off somewhere. I could feel heat and sensed hot sand and danger. I could hear my name being called and I started to feel quite alarmed as I felt myself drifting off. I grabbed the arm of my friend and told him to hold onto me tight. After a few moments the strange feeling left me and I returned to normality – and quickly reached for a glass of wine.

Several weeks later the engineer who had accompanied me on that business trip looked up the leader of the film crew when he next visited the United States and he found out the possible cause of my distress. The crew had been planning to film the supposed site of Noah's Ark – someone had told them of its location on the border between Turkey and Iraq. After their delay they eventually found their way down to the border and were in the process of making their film when they were challenged by Iraqi border guards. After some heated exchanges they started to shoot at them and the young man who owned the necklace had been caught in crossfire and was pinned down behind some rocks for some time. Eventually they all managed to escape but it had been an extremely frightening experience for them all.

We believe the young American was clutching the necklace and using it as an amulet and somehow he had made a connection with me on the night of the attack. This whole episode made me realise that not only do objects have 'memories' – but they can also link people, no matter where they are.

As I became more experienced with healing so did my ability to identify and handle the energies that attach to objects. One day a woman visited me who was convinced that a younger woman had entranced her husband. Despite having been a completely devoted husband and father, he had fallen in love with this young woman and started having an affair with her. His behaviour had become erratic and his character seemed to have changed almost overnight. Other catastrophic events had occurred in the wife's life around this time. A cooker in her apartment had suddenly gone up in flames for no accountable reason and she had also suffered an unexpected miscarriage. Understandably, she was most distressed. She brought me a picture of her husband and I felt that the energies around him were dark and heavy.

Using distance healing, I cleared the energies around both the husband and his wife, but I sensed something else was affecting her so I also visited her apartment to see if there were any objects that may have been planted to bring her bad luck. Opening myself to the energies of the apartment and using my hands, I searched for anything that might be the cause of her problems. Eventually I came across a painting that the couple had brought with them when they had moved from East Africa.

I sensed strong negative energy vibrations coming from the painting and again experienced the sensation of cobwebs and 'spookiness' that comes from spells. I closed my eyes and using inner sight saw a line leading from the painting back to a large African man – a witchdoctor. He was enormous, and had a jolly face and a huge grin.

I asked him if he had put a spell on the painting. He said yes, he most certainly had. I asked him if he would take it back and he laughed and said, 'Why not, I've been paid and I can now use it again.' I was amazed. The energies lifted and the room cleared.

At the time I just acted spontaneously, but with hindsight I wouldn't return a spell like that again. First, I wouldn't know what to expect when I followed an energy stream back to its source – it may be far more powerful and overwhelming than the witchdoctor and I might be unable to perform the clearing. Second, I didn't like the idea that the source might use a spell on someone else. I didn't find out who had put the spell on the family but the woman suspected a business rival of her husband. After some time she and her husband moved back into harmony and she seemed much happier the last time I spoke to her.

Although most people won't ever suffer a curse, many of us experience times when we may be surrounded by people who either don't like or respect us or are downright hostile. The effects of their thoughts and attitudes can be similar to that of being cursed and will drain us of our energy. These bad vibes affect us mentally, making us depressed, ill at ease and very often fatigued. We all need a good strong flow of positive and light energy to sustain us. In fact, we can also become physically ill if our energy levels dip drastically and our immune systems are affected.

In Chapter 3 I will explain why we are so affected by other people's emotions and thoughts, and I will look at ways in which we can immunise ourselves from them. If you are affected by strong negativity caused by curses, spells and the harmful thoughts of others you will find more powerful protection and help in Chapter 7.

Positive and Negative Earth Energies

Since I left the Far East and came back to live in Britain I have become aware of another source of negative energy that can create anything from discomfort to serious illness for some people. There are circumstances when our natural environment may be the cause of our distress.

All living things are surrounded by an energy field, which we call an aura, and the planet Earth is no exception. The Earth's magnetic field can be disturbed and it shows signs of stress in the misalignment of energies. This negative Earth energy is referred to as 'geopathic stress' and it can be the cause of negativity in and around your home and workplace.

There are a number of ways to identify this Earth energy and find where it is strong – whether it is positive or negative – and later in the book we will be looking at ways to counteract the harm and disturbance that negative Earth energy can bring (see Chapter 6). I used one of these methods on my home in Burley, which is in the centre of the New Forest in Hampshire, England.

Burley is famous for its witches and even in the 1950s a white witch called Sybil lived in the village. She was renowned for her good spells and herbal magic. Unfortunately, she was harried by the press and sensationalised by the media to the point that she left England and set up home in the United States, where she flourished and became very well known for her healing. It was our loss, but today the village is full of gift shops that sell gifts and knick-knacks relating to witchcraft.

After reading about the energy lines ('ley lines') that criss-cross the Earth, one day a group of us went into my garden to see if there was a powerful energy line crossing the land. I am delighted to say that we found a strong positive force that ran diagonally across my house, and when I checked it on the map I found it was part of the line that links Avebury, Stonehenge and Salisbury Cathedral, all exceptional sacred sites with enormous energy forces. I am convinced that I was led to my home because of this alignment when we were house-hunting in the New Forest six years ago. I felt a strong urge to see this particular house and when I came close to it I felt a tremendous surge of energy – which I call a 'whoosh' – as I approached our drive for the first time.

The entire purchase went incredibly smoothly and we have been extremely happy and peaceful in the house since the day we bought it. I often use my home for energy workshops and during these gatherings we have some amazing experiences that I am sure are mainly due to the wonderful location of the house and the energy that flows through it. I also use the house for healing sessions, which again I am certain are helped by the strong positive energy force in the house.

I am fortunate that the energy line that crosses my house is positively charged so it brings uplifting and invigorating energy, but there are situations where a line can become distorted and misaligned, thus affecting any building erected over it. For example, if there have been major road works or a large building has been constructed on a powerful positive line, the disturbance to the Earth's natural flow by the intrusion can turn the energy from positive to negative. This natural energy disturbance, or geopathic stress, can have a detrimental outcome on the health of those living or working in the vicinity.

With the rise of the electronic age we are also surrounded by detrimental electrical energies from microwaves, mobile phones and so on. These hazards of modern-day living, which are commonly referred to as 'electromagnetic stress', are not only in our homes but surround us and contaminate our environment. For example, we are affected by the emissions from electricity pylons and substations and microwave mobile phone masts.

Long-term effects of negative Earth energies

There is no doubt that if we are exposed to negative energies over a prolonged period we will be affected. I recently visited my goddaughter Katy, who was suffering from a bout of depression and had returned to the family home to recover. There were several reasons for her illness but one of the contributing factors was the low temperature of her own house, where she felt cold all the time. I asked her if this was just a natural chill from an underheated house, or whether she felt that the house was maybe affected by a presence.

Katy is a healer and a psychic herself so we could talk about this without her getting spooked! She said that the heating system was inadequate but also admitted that she *was* aware of a presence in the house. She had sensed it wandering around upstairs, making her feel uneasy at times. She also admitted that she had been feeling tired for some time before her illness – in fact since she had moved to her new home. So while her father organised new central heating and solved the problem on a purely physical level, I thought it would be a good idea for me to investigate the energies of her house as well.

I went to the house with her and checked for the detrimental influences of electromagnetic stress – from any pylons, substations and so on near the house – and found it clear. I then checked to see if there were any Earth energy lines that could be disturbing the harmony of the home and found one negative line that ran right through her bedroom. This was the worst possible place as she would have been in its influence for long periods of time while sleeping. We also then found that the same line ran under the chair that she used downstairs. Using methods that I will share with you later in this book, I cleared the line and turned it to its original positive state. I then checked for the presence of a spirit in the house.

I should mention at this point that I use dowsing to look for all forms of negative energy. Dowsing is the ancient practice of locating objects, water, oil or practically anything that is unseen because it is beneath the Earth or out of sight for some reason. You can connect to the vibrations of what you are seeking by the use of divining rods or a pendulum and find it by reading the movement of the dowsing object. It is a skill that anyone can acquire with practice and patience and I will give you full instructions on how to do this in Chapter 6.

Back in Katy's house, I found the presence of a young boy and gently sent him from the house and on to the spirit world where he belonged. Katy actually felt him leaving because the energy surrounding him was cold and depressing and he took it with him as he moved out of the house and passed right by where she was standing. The house instantly became warmer and lighter, and by the time I had blessed it and filled it with uplifting energies it felt completely different – light and bright, and friendly and inviting. So with her father's new heating system, my energy-clearing and the repainting of her lounge by her mother and stepfather, Katy's home received not only a detox but a complete change of energy.

I strongly recommend that if you are suffering from depression or lack of energy, one aspect of your life that you should look at is the energy of your house. If your home feels unnaturally cold and unfriendly, or even if some parts of the house seem to be dark and uninviting, you should consider giving it a cleansing too.

How Do We Manage Negative Energies?

Although most people don't have daily experiences of haunting spirits, many of us have come across one form of negative energy or another in our lives. Some of these are obvious no matter how sensitive or insensitive we may feel we are. Most of us have felt cold shivers when entering old and abandoned buildings, or had butterflies in the pits of our stomachs when someone had been angry and shouted at us. These are both instances of picking up on negative energy and there are several other types of harmful energy that can be a problem to us and our health.

A lack of positive energy can also cause problems. For instance, another form of high-vibration energy is sunlight and we all thrive in a light environment. But some people are seriously affected by a lack of sunlight, especially in the winter months, and suffer from depression and lassitude – a syndrome called Seasonal Affective Disorder (SAD). So whether we are aware of it or not, we are all affected by the state of the energy that surrounds us.

Apart from external sources of negative energy I have found that no matter where I am in the world the greatest threats to our peace of mind and harmony are the thoughts and attitudes of other people. A person with a negative attitude to life can drain us of our own energy more quickly than anything. We will look at ways in which we can identify the effects people have on us, how we should respond to them and how we can protect ourselves from these influences. Of course, our own downbeat and pessimistic thoughts can also de-energise us very effectively as well.

My main task as a healer is to clear the energy blockages caused by difficult experiences, conditioning, set attitudes, anxieties, and other negative emotions and thoughts. I have found that although I can clear these blocks for a while, if a person persists with the same behaviour and attitudes and refuses to take responsibility for their own life and healing, then within a few months they will be back with a similar problem. So helping people to heal themselves has become one of my main objectives.

Before we look at all the sources of negativity that we cannot control, let's first look at those that we create ourselves and learn to control them and bring them to heel. With this in mind, the next chapter is concerned with ways in which you can generate positive rather than negative energies yourself, with the power of *your* mind and *your* will and *your* intent. So let's begin our clearing and cleansing by looking at how our own negative thoughts and emotions affect us – and how we can manage them.

2

Overcoming Self-negativity

In this chapter I shall look at the way our own personal energy system works and why we are so receptive to the levels of energy around us. I shall also explain how you can create your own depression and deplete your valuable life force with your thoughts and attitudes. I will look at the many ways that you can uplift yourself and raise your energy levels.

What Does Negative Energy Feel Like?

When I first started healing I couldn't identify the blocks and negativity in a person's energy at all. I did all my healing with the faith that something good was going to come of it. However, eventually I did begin to feel the negative energies. The best way I can describe them is that they are 'sticky' and 'heavy'. I also often get negative 'whooshes', which feel like being covered in cobwebs, and sometimes I experience the prickling sensation of darkness and evil that you may get when watching a horror film.

When negative energies combine they can be a powerful force, as I once experienced conclusively while I was staying with a girl friend in Kuala Lumpur in Malaysia. We had been having great fun all week with her recent purchase, a set of crystal bowls. These are made from tiny chips of crystal and vary in size from about twelve inches to twenty-four inches in diameter. When a leather-covered stick is rubbed around the rim they send out amazing reverberations that are great for raising energies and healing.

All week we had been filling the house with waves and waves of tremendous sound. That night we had invited around the local Hearts and Hands group. Hearts and Hands is an organisation that I founded to promote natural healing, and we meet regularly in groups to heal one another and anyone we know who is sick, and to send healing thoughts and love to humanity, animals and our world. That night we had a great turnout of nearly fifty people.

We had finished a meditation and I performed healing for everyone present, releasing and clearing their negativity and energy blocks. We were relaxing afterwards with drinks and cake when one of the women started to play one of the crystal bowls. After about thirty seconds there was a loud bang and a crash and the entire bowl burst into fragments.

Everyone stopped dead still, completely mesmerised by the intensity of the sound. I was the only one who moved – I was drawn towards the bowl. As I leant down over it a great force hit me in the chest, knocking me back. The force then flew through the room, knocking another girl off her feet and winding her, and hitting the arm of a man before it left through the window.

People rushed to me asking if I had had a heart attack. No – it was the force of the ball of negative energy that had collected in the bowl as a result of the healing. Normally I have a bowl of salt water in the room when I do energy clearing because salt mops up negative energies, but that day I had forgotten. As a result, the crystal had attracted the negativity and held it, and when someone started to play it, it had gone into overload – the bowl had shattered and the energy ball had flown free.

For some days afterwards I had a bruise on my chest as a result of its onslaught and I learnt to have a very healthy respect for the power and force of negative energy. Let me reassure you that this was an exceptional experience and I will be showing you ways of protecting yourself throughout this book – you won't need a bullet-proof vest.

Energy – What Is It?

Before we go any further into 'negative' and 'positive' energies and how they affect us, let's start by looking at what energy and energy fields really are. I must admit that I didn't pay a great deal of attention to my physics teacher at school. I started to fall behind the week we covered density, when we were introduced to formulae and equations.

My inability to hold numbers in my head – I still have a problem with phone numbers and bank balances – resulted in mental shutdown. So when my editor suggested that I should include a description of energy my stomach did a flip. I can tell you what energy *feels* like. I can describe the difference between positive and negative energy. I can tell you how to clear negative energy. But to give you a *scientific* explanation – well, that might be stretching me a little too far.

However, my father taught me a great lesson: when you need to learn something new or understand something that isn't clear – buy a book. So I bought *Six Easy Pieces*, a layperson's guide to physics by Richard P. Feynman, a leading physicist of our times. It's a pretty little book and I grasped it with glee when I saw it on the shelf of a bookshop at Heathrow airport. Great inflight reading for my holiday – it was so small and attractive. I thought that this would answer all my questions with ease.

Well, after the first six pages the book began to get a bit technical – those formulae again – but it felt good to have the author confirm facts that I knew from my ex-periences as a healer. I have always known that although we humans seem to be solid and dense matter we are made of tiny particles that are each surrounded by an energy field. We are, in fact, completely made of energy and as such each of us is a changing, moving mass.

I also perceive this to be true of all things in nature, whether it is a plant or a pebble, and it was great to read and confirm this too. To quote Richard Feynman: 'All things are made of atoms – little particles that move around in perpetual motion.' He goes on to say: 'In that one sentence, you will see, there is an enormous amount of information about the world, if just a little imagination and thinking are applied.' We can follow his advice – with a bit of imagination we can understand from this scientific fact that everything in nature has both a life form and energy.

Another thing Richard Feynman says is that 'we have no knowledge what energy *is*'. Wonderful, I am not as stupid as I thought – if a Nobel Prize-winning scientist doesn't know, what chance have I got? However, he does go on to say that energy is measurable, in watts and thermal units and so on, and that it can never disappear. It can change form – for instance from heat to light – but it can never disperse completely. So if you start with six units of energy you will end up with six units of energy.

So let's take these two basic scientific facts – that all matter is energy and that it will never disperse (it can change form but will always be there) – and apply them to ourselves and our human form.

Auras

Since every particle – every atom, every cell – of our body is surrounded by an energy field, our entire body is also therefore surrounded by a field of energy. This field is called the 'aura' and it spreads to about an arm's length all around our body.

The aura's general appearance is illustrated on the following page. Also shown are the channels called 'meridians', which are responsible for conveying energy around our body to feed different parts of it. The meridians are discussed in more detail on page 37.

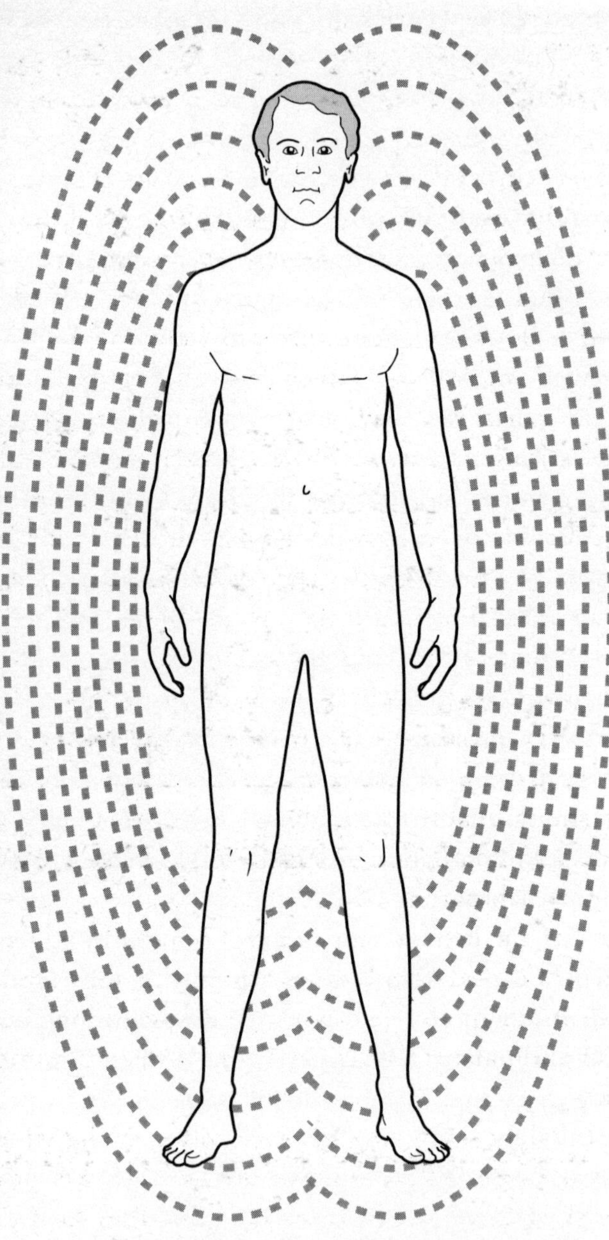

The aura of the human body, also showing the energy meridians.

The aura has a series of 'bodies' or layers – spiritual, mental, emotional, and physical. All but the last are etheric – that is, they cannot be seen by the human eye because they are less dense than our physical body. However, they are all there and they are all very real. They all have a huge impact on each other and they need to be treated together if we are to become truly well, truly healed.

Energy flows around our physical body following channels called 'meridians', which feed all our major organs and body parts. It's essential for good health that this flow is kept strong and clear, for as soon as any part of our being becomes depleted we are likely to have problems. These problems can manifest physically, mentally or emotionally. Our spiritual state affects our mental state and our mental state affects our energetic state and our energetic state affects our physical state. Our well-being moves from top to bottom and from inside out.

One of the reasons why people are becoming a little disillusioned with their visits to the local doctor is that he or she is unable, through lack of time, to give truly holistic, or total, healing. Often with just five minutes to spare for each patient, the doctor is inclined to give us a 'quick fix' medicinal cure that will hopefully correct the physical body balance. Unfortunately, this solves only the surface problem and unless we go deeper in our healing to clear and balance our entire being, we can become sick again.

Fortunately, over the last few years ancient healing processes from different cultures have become popular in the West. They are all holistic in that they heal all our bodies – spiritual, mental, emotional and physical – and most of them are focused on clearing and releasing the flow of the aura. Shiatsu, reflexology, acupuncture, acupressure, cranio-sacral therapy, Reiki and Indian head massage all work either directly or indirectly on the meridians to keep the essential life force flowing through and around the body.

The aura's changing colour

Let's look a little closer now at the aura, for it is the barometer of our spiritual health and emotional well-being. Our aura is constantly changing and every thought and emotion that we experience affects both its shape and colour. When we are depressed the colour of our aura will appear muddy, reflecting our bleak mood. When we are bright and happy then our aura too will appear bright and shining. If our aura is purple around our head it shows that we are spiritually aware. A lot of yellow in our aura indicates that we are energised, red can be a sign of anger or passion, blue of intuition – and so on.

Some people can actually see our aura and how it is altered by our mood and emotional state. However, to most of us it will usually be invisible, and if you want to see your aura for yourself I would suggest that you have a photograph taken using the Kirlian process. This was developed in Russia specifically to register the human energy field on film.

You will find Kirlian cameras in many mind, body and spirit shops, and also at psychic and natural health fairs and festivals. All Kirlian photographs come with an interpretation of the colours and what they depict. Just remember that the colours you will see in the photo are not permanent – as your mood changes so does the colour of your aura.

The aura and vibrations

Energy can also be perceived as either 'thin' or 'dense'. Despite losing my way in the density classes at school I did at least manage to take on board the fact that a cork is less dense than lead. But rather than discuss the formulae to show the relative density of matter, let's talk about the vibrations instead. High vibration is less dense than low vibration. Light is high vibration and dark is low vibration, so if our aura is light then we are in a state of high vibration. Emotions can also be classified in this way – love is high vibration and hate is low vibration.

These emotional vibrations then connect with our mental and spiritual state. So if we are feeling spiritually 'connected' and in touch with the love of the universe our aura will shine forth brightly – which is why the halos depicted in paintings of spiritual masters, saints and angels are shown as gold or translucent. Similarly, if our mind perceives something as an obstacle this may impact on our emotions, making us feel anxious and giving us a dull aura – and perhaps also causing us a physical reaction like an upset stomach. Positive energy sets off positive reactions in our aura, and vice versa with negative energy. In this book you will learn both how to increase positive experiences and how to manage negative ones.

When we talk about negative energy we associate it with darkness, low vibration and density. When I am healing someone I will pick up negativity by touch and sense. I feel the low vibrations as 'sticky' and heavy. To be a healer you need to be reasonably light yourself and through this you can sense the difference between high and low vibrations. A person who is, say, a murderer and lives in a constant state of darkness and negativity will not be able to sense the light as well as someone who follows a more spiritual and lighter path through life. This is because a person who is able to perform cruel and abusive acts towards others has closed down a great part of their sensitivity and emotions. A kind, empathic and compassionate person will be more open and tuned in to the needs and wants of others and will therefore be more sensitive.

If you find that you are sensitive and your sensitivity causes you problems at times, then keep on reading, because throughout the book I will be showing you ways in which you can protect yourself without losing your ability to be empathic towards others. I will show you how you can effectively put a 'shield' around your aura so that you can avoid being affected by the lower vibrations in your surroundings.

The aura's changing shape

Generally our aura surrounds us to a distance of about six feet and is usually egg-shaped. However, the shape and size will be affected by our mood – for example, if we are having a bad day and feeling low or depressed our aura will come in closer to our body and be less vibrant. Similarly if we are introspective and withdrawn into ourselves our aura will be smaller. It will expand as we feel inspired and more outgoing, so when an actor is in full flow on the stage, putting his all into the part he is playing, or a singer is singing with all her heart and soul, you would see a full and glowing aura surrounding them.

If we are let down by someone our energy will drop and our aura will deflate – in fact we talk about 'going down like a pricked balloon'. On the other hand, if we let our ego take over we become 'over-inflated' – just ready for someone to get out their pin. If we hear bad news or have a shock – 'a blow to the stomach' – our aura will become dented at our solar plexus. If we are threatened we will try to protect ourselves by retracting our aura and mentally strengthening its outer rim by sending out defiant spikes of energy.

Our energy field is also affected by our health and general well-being. If we are sick our aura will be depleted, as will our total energy source. When we are in full health it will grow. If we become unfocused and allow our mind to flit from subject to subject our aura will mirror this and will become depleted and scattered. When we are stressed we are often in this scattered state – not able to concentrate because we have too much on our mind. This is why stress is so harmful to us – as our mind skips around so our energies skip too, leaving us drained.

Have you ever associated your low energy with the fact that you are not focused? Have you noticed that when you spend the day starting but not finishing things – jumping from job to job or subject to subject – you are exhausted by the evening? Your energy field will be darting in and out following your thoughts and becoming depleted as it does so. If you could see your aura it would appear something like an octopus with tentacles in many directions. The most spectacular version of this is the shape our aura adopts when we are hysterical – with energy flying out all over the place like a firework.

So our experiences, thoughts, attitudes and emotions all affect the shape, form and colour of our energy field, which, although not obvious to the naked eye, we may all sense with our 'inner sight' and our intuition – that inner knowledge we have that cannot be explained by logic. In our everyday lives we can often find that people around us don't even have to speak for us to sense when they are negative or positive. Intuitively perceiving their aura, we may describe them as being spiky, down, in a dark mood, beside themselves, or glowing, bright, larger than life, soft – and so on.

Ways to lighten your aura

If you feel that you need a pick-me-up to brighten and lift yourself, here are a number of 'quick fixes' you can use to lighten your aura.

EXERCISE: A MINI-MEDITATION TO BRING IN LIGHT

- Find a quiet space and make yourself comfortable. If you are sitting on a chair, place your feet firmly on the ground.
- Breathe in deeply several times.
- Imagine a bright stream of light coming down from the sky and entering the top of your head.
- Sense the light filling your entire body.
- Now see the light filling your aura and turning it bright gold.
- Sit for a few minutes and know that you are completely surrounded by gold light.

EXERCISE: TAKE AN ENERGY SHOWER

- When you stand under the shower imagine that the water is clearing away all negativity and filling your aura with light.
- See all your cares and worries being washed away down the drain.
- Stand for a few minutes and enjoy the sensation of your entire being becoming cleansed and totally clear and fresh.

- Sense that your aura is now sparkling and clear.

EXERCISE: SWEEPING YOUR AURA

This is part of the aura-clearing process that I will be showing you later in this chapter. You can use this method to quickly smooth away any 'spikes' and 'ruffles' in your aura and make you feel more together and calmer.

- Using your hands as a comb, sweep through your aura, starting above your head.
- Sweep down around your entire body.
- Do this for about two minutes.

Our Thoughts are Energy

So we are now aware that our physical bodies are made of constantly moving matter that is energy, and that we are constantly outputting energy of one form or another. The vibration of the energy we create depends on how positive or negative our thoughts are. Our thoughts too are energy and their vibration is carried to whatever our thoughts are focused on. If I am thinking kind and loving thoughts about my husband then as he is the focus of my thought he will receive the energy of my thought. Loving thoughts are high-vibration thoughts, so he will receive a stream of high-vibration uplifting energy and this will obviously make him feel good. If he is depressed, my positive thoughts directed at him can help to lift his spirits and his depression. So when someone is sick we must make sure that we don't worry about them or visualise them being ill as this will only make then worse.

Once we receive energy from a person's thoughts we can use it for whatever purpose suits us. If we are sick we may use the energy to heal ourselves, as we usually have low energy resources when we are ill and the creation of new cells and cellular repair work both need energy to be successful. Of course, all this will be going on at an unconscious level, and we will just feel better in ourselves. This is the basis of distance healing, where we can send help to people far away just by thinking well of them.

The effects of thoughts

Every single thought we have has an effect on someone or something. This statement follows the rules of physics – it takes us back to Richard Feynman's point that energy cannot disappear and you always finish up with the same amount of energy at the end that you had at the start. The energy may have moved away and it may have changed vibration, but it will still exist.

All day long you are taking energy from your energy store and moving it and changing it. With every thought you are either transforming negative energy into positive energy or positive into negative, or making positive situations even better or negative situations even worse. If you are helping someone or simply thinking well of them you will feel good yourself – not just from the satisfaction and fulfilment that comes from giving help to others but also because your own vibrations will rise as you generate and transfer positive energy through your field. You will also have raised the vibrations of the person you have helped.

If on the other hand you are upset with someone and are thinking badly of them, then your negative thoughts will harm both yourself and the other person. Whenever you think of someone your energy passes to their own energy body like a stream and attaches to it. So it is so important for your own welfare and the welfare of those close to you that you watch your thoughts and actions and, wherever possible, keep them positive.

Thought Forms

If we consistently have negative thoughts we eventually create a negative 'thought form' – a mass of dense, low-vibration negative thought-energy created when individual negative thoughts combine to form a 'lump'. It's not easy to describe, but imagine a tangled mass of wool. Its density depends on how negative the thoughts were that created it. A thought form will sit in our aura and as it becomes more solid it will eventually bring down the level of our auric energy and hamper the natural and healthy flow of energy around our body. In fact we will be congesting our aura with our thoughts.

Thought forms also obstruct the flow of the energy through the meridians and so are often also referred to as blocks. If you are an artist or writer you may have suffered the dreaded experience of sitting in front of a blank piece of paper – or nowadays a clear computer screen – and waiting for inspiration to pour forth. When we are still uninspired after hours of trying we call this writer's or artist's block – something that most authors, students, journalists and artists will have experienced, most likely more than once!

Thought forms are normally created by persistent worry and anxiety. In the case of writer's block it is probably the fear of non-achieving that sets up a negative thought form and stops the energy flowing to our brain and stimulating our creativity. If there are times when you struggle for inspiration you may get some help from the process of clearing thought forms outlined later in this chapter.

Thought forms and health

One of the significant sources of illness and poor well-being is lack of energy, and this can be caused by a negative thought-form. All the organs of our body need to vibrate at a certain level for their continued vitality and health, so if their energy levels drop significantly the cells will start to sicken. If life-force energy cannot reach a part of our body then we will eventually become sick. We will start by suffering fatigue, then we will become depressed and despondent. As the energy of our organs becomes depleted we will become physically ill.

A simple and common example of a thought form harming our health is when stress causes a headache. When we consistently worry about something or fear something we create a particular thought form that sits above our head – and before long it weighs down on us and gives us a headache.

What causes us to create negative thought forms?

If you are experiencing any of the following there is a good chance that your energy levels are being depleted and that you are creating negative thought forms:

- **Lethargy** Do you feel that everything is too much trouble? Do you want to be left alone to vegetate?
- **Headaches** Some headaches are a symptom of a lack of energy. Do you have a heavy, 'muzzy' head and find it difficult to get your thoughts together and focused?

- **Depression** Do you feel low in spirit and find it difficult to get excited or inspired about anything? Do you want to sleep in all the time rather than get up and get on with your life? Do you suffer a lack of enthusiasm?
- **Low immune system** Are you always catching colds and flu and the latest virus?

Let's now look in more detail at some of the causes of the persistent negative thoughts that create potentially harmful thought forms.

Stress

These days it is quite normal to suffer from stress. Or to put it another way – these days many of us allow ourselves to become stressed. What is stress? It's a state we experience when we are finding it difficult to be calm throughout the day. We become agitated and anxious. Our heartbeat and pulse rise and our adrenaline rushes through our body. Years ago we would usually have had these responses in our bodies only when we were in physical danger. Now we can get them just by getting stuck in a traffic jam.

Obviously it is not healthy for our bodies to suffer stress every day. We tense our muscles and this creates pain centres, often in our shoulders and neck. Migraine headaches are a notable result of stress. Our stomachs take the full brunt of the adrenaline rushes and we often suffer nervous ailments like Irritable Bowel Syndrome, candida, peptic ulcers, constipation and poor digestion. We also suffer mentally and keep going over the possible outcomes and issues of our lives until we find that we are constantly 'hyper' or desperately tired.

One of the results of stress is that we constantly have anxious thoughts that we repeat over and over – like 'I shall be late for this deadline', 'I won't succeed in this project', 'my daughter is going to fail her exam', or 'I know this person is going to annoy me'.

Everyone is prone to stress. It's not just the domain of businessmen and women. Whatever your occupation and circumstances you are likely to get stressed at some time. For example, most of us get uptight at some stage when travelling, whether it's waiting for a delayed train, being caught in an interminable traffic jam, having difficulty finding a parking spot or going through the processes of modern air travel.

Some of us are stretched too thinly. Nowadays we may 'wear many hats' in our working lives and have several responsibilities – especially working mothers or single parents, who must try to balance their lives between family and work. This creates anxieties and the endless worry – 'am I giving enough time to my family/work?' Such constant thoughts will create negative thought forms that will lodge in our aura.

Prevent stress – learn to relax

In this section we are looking at a number of methods that we can use to clear ourselves of negativity, so let's look at how we can prevent stress. The cure for stress is to learn to relax and go with the flow. As stress creates in us the feeling that we are about to run a marathon, with all our muscles in 'go!' mode, we need to use the antidote of complete relaxation.

I use meditation, aromatherapy massages, yoga and exercise to help me. Other people find listening to music and reading helpful and my husband manages to chill out completely by watching the television. I personally find there is too much verbal or physical violence in most programmes – whether it be the news, a film or a soap opera – to make this a relaxing pastime. Whatever you use as the key to unwind, make sure that you allocate time for it, as stress can cause you harm in the long run if it's not managed.

Taking a little more laid-back approach to life will also help. Try to stop yourself from worrying about future events, for by worrying you are living a negative experience before it happens. So if it does happen – and it might not – you will have lived it twice, before the event and during it.

Concentrate on the present and let the future look after itself. Go with the flow a little – whenever you are affected by things out of your control, like a delayed train or traffic jam, learn to see that your stress cannot help. Work on the basis that these delays are meant to be. Which they are – they may be there to teach you patience or they may have occurred to delay you for some other reason that you can't see immediately. I usually see travel delays as a way of avoiding some trouble, for example an accident. So just use the extra time the delay has given you on the journey to contemplate something positive in your life or plan a special event.

Make a determined effort to release stress from your life. I suggest you check out that you are in the right job. Do you find that your work makes you feel good about yourself or are you struggling to manage a position that just doesn't suit your temperament? You may think that it's impossible to live without stress. I even know several people who are quite addicted to the adrenaline rush and I certainly think that I was at one time in my business career. I know I enjoyed the thrill of rushing around, chasing deadlines and pushing myself to my limit. Thank goodness I have learnt to slow down a little now. At least I have learnt to switch off so that my body and mind have time to recover. If you are an adrenaline junkie you may have to master this aspect of yourself like any other form of addiction.

Low Self-esteem

Through our conditioning and experiences we may have developed negative thought forms that lead us to low self-esteem, which in turn can result in further negative thought forms and negative behaviour patterns. I will take a look now at some of the origins of negative mind-sets that you may have adopted in your life and what low self-respect can lead to. I will then show you some ways in which you can start to overcome these negative attitudes towards yourself.

Conditioning by our culture, society and family

As we go through life we adopt attitudes and limitations from our culture, religion, society and family. These thoughts and conditionings can cohere into mindsets – fixed ways of thinking that can limit our freedom and constrain our lives. They can become shackles that hold us back from enjoying and living life to the full, binding our minds and our spirit in negative thought patterns such as 'I can't do that' or 'I'm not good enough for this'.

Now is a good time to take a clear look at your upbringing and see if your own attitudes and mindset have been affected by your culture, religion, parents or schooling, or by the media.

- Were you chastised for lack of performance in your youth?
- Do you now never believe that your work is good enough?
- Do you consider financial success the yardstick for your personal success?
- Do you find fault in your figure or body?
- Do you constantly feel guilty for one reason or another?

If you answer 'yes' to any of these questions it indicates that you have been affected by the mindsets of others and this may mean you have created negative attitudes towards yourself. Write down all the negative attitudes you think you have developed and see if you can find the cause of them.

Throughout your life you may have created a perception of yourself based on the words and actions of others. Dominant, intolerant or impatient parents, teachers, peers and siblings may have suggested to you that you are slow, lazy, arrogant, unintelligent and so on. You may also have had some negative experiences like failing an exam, losing a job or losing a girlfriend/boyfriend to a more 'attractive' rival. You may have taken all these experiences to heart and decided that you are not worthy of success, love or happiness. Over the years you may have gradually lost your self-esteem. Even now you may find that you don't like yourself very much, especially if you always compare yourself with others. So you may also have lost your self-respect.

It's not difficult in this open and communicating world to see and hear of those who excel at any aspect of life. Winners are lauded through the media and it's difficult to avoid their success. There is nothing wrong with this, but if you constantly compare yourself and your achievements to them you can end up perceiving that you are a 'failure' or 'second class'. Once you lose your self-respect you are then liable to treat yourself as unsuccessful, as a loser. When we have low self-esteem we may stop loving ourselves and eventually start to abuse ourselves. Ask yourself right now if you consider yourself to be worthy of love. Also see if any of the following negative patterns are present in your life:

- Dependency on drugs or alcohol.
- Choosing partners who do not respect you – even abuse you emotionally or physically.
- Being in a job that gives you no satisfaction or feelings of achievement.
- Neglecting yourself physically through a lack of exercise, poor eating habits, and so on.

If you can see any of the above patterns in your life then the chances are you have low self-esteem. If so it is time to start to work on loving yourself:

- Intend that you will, right from this moment, look for your good points rather than the bad.
- Realise that you are as worthy of love – from yourself as well as from others – as anyone else.
- Take a positive attitude towards yourself.
- Follow the methods to be positive at the end of this chapter and make them a part of your daily life.

Addiction

Let's look a little closer at addiction now. It goes hand in hand with all sorts of negative feelings, aspects and situations and can be one of the results of years of low self-esteem and lack of self-respect. It can be really destructive not only for yourself but also for those around you. I am not qualified to help you if you have a full-blown addiction to hard drugs but I would say that if you can get everything else in order through the suggestions in this book, you may find it a little easier to take command of your life again.

The following example is quite typical of the sort of addiction that troubles so many of us. I was giving a workshop on healing in Johannesburg, South Africa. One of the women at the workshop was addicted to Coke – the liquid kind. She couldn't get through a day without several cans of Coca-Cola. I don't know what it was in the Coke that had her hooked – maybe it was the caffeine, maybe it was the sugar, anyway she couldn't give it up.

Two things bother most of us who have such an addiction and she was no exception. One is that the substance to which we are addicted – for example, tobacco, alcohol, sugar, chocolate, Coca-Cola – may be potentially harmful in large quantities. The second aspect is that our addiction is a sign of weakness and the fact that we can't live without the substance shows a lack of control on our behalf. The addiction can become a negative force in our life. One of the energetic results of addictions is that the brain keeps sending out the 'demand' messages and these become a thought form.

The woman with the Coke addiction offered to be the guinea pig for my healing demonstration. In the group there was another lady who had been a powerful clairvoyant but was disappointed as her gift seemed to have left her and she was hoping that by attending this course she could find it again. As I was working on my patient, this other lady suddenly looked over and said we needed to clear behind her head and went to a spot on the right-hand side of the woman's head. I put my hand there and felt the sticky energy of a negative thought form. This was the thought form of the girl's addiction and as we cleared it away we shifted the need that it was creating. She managed to give up Coke after that. The other lady went on to recover all her clairvoyant gifts – so two happy customers!

Experiences that Create Negative Emotions

Some of our negative responses to life come as a direct result of our personal experiences. Of course, this doesn't make them less harmful to us but it does make them understandable. I am referring especially to traumatic or disturbing situations that leave their mark on us long after the event in the form of emotional and mental scars. The following are just a few of the experiences that take their toll on our emotional and mental well-being:

- Loss of a close family member.
- Childhood abuse and lack of love from the family.
- Rape or abuse by a stranger.
- Physical disablement.

Loss of a close family member

If we lose someone close to us early in life it can leave us with feelings of abandonment. This loss can be through death, divorce or deliberate avoidance. We can then feel insecure later in life. This can result in us being fearful of making close relationships in case we are let down again. Remember that unless we open ourselves to love we minimise our chances of having a fulfilling and satisfying relationship whether it be with a partner, children or friends. Remember that the experience of closeness and sharing with someone we have lost is something precious that we can treasure always. The memories of tenderness and love can never be taken from you – they have become a part of you.

Childhood abuse and lack of love from the family

This is another situation that can break down our trust. It can make us bitter and fearful of relationships. It will often leave us with a feeling of being dirty, of being worthless and not deserving of love. Remember that you are a unique and spiritual being who deserves as much love as the next person. You are not to blame for things which, because you were a child, you were powerless to prevent. You should aim to shed any guilt as it will become your straitjacket in life, preventing you from having the happiness and love you deserve. You can also break the cycle that so often occurs when a child is abused. Work hard at showing love to your own children – it's not enough to feel the love, you need to show it too.

Rape or abuse by a stranger

Again this brings up a question of trust. It brings fear of the outside world and can lower your self-esteem and self-worth. But it is possible not to let the event ruin your life. The experience was terrible but again you are in no way to blame. Your assailant released a deep negative energy upon you but you were not its cause. You were just in the wrong place at the wrong time. You may become a lifelong victim and your aggressor the lifetime winner if you don't let it go and move on. Of course, great strength and courage are needed to rid yourself of this negative event – use whatever healing you can find to help yourself. As with all these experiences acceptance is the key to releasing the past.

Physical disablement

I know of two young men who have been struck down in the prime of life. One, a dear friend of mine called Apuu, was a jockey who was thrown and broke his neck in one of his first professional races. To be a jockey was his life's dream – it was to be the means to take him and his family out of poverty and was his way to success. He is now a quadriplegic and hasn't been able to walk since the accident.

Understandably, Apuu spent some time in a very depressed state. But he retained just a little movement in his arms and learnt to use a computer to write, and the last time I saw him he was able to move his fingers a little and was starting to draw. Apuu always has the most enormous smile on his face and he is an absolute inspiration to all who know him.

The other young man is Victor Vermeulen, a good friend of a friend of mine. He has been quadriplegic since he broke his neck in a swimming pool just as he was chosen to play cricket for his province in South Africa. At the time he was rated the best up-and-coming cricketer in the country and would certainly have been selected to play for the national cricket team – his life's dream. Due to the tragic murder of his father he also needed his work to support himself and his mother.

Victor now gives inspirational talks throughout South Africa, letting his words and his courage show others the way to being the 'victor' over difficult circumstances. He has also written a book, *The Victor Within* (see Further Reading, page 282), which tells how he overcame the limitations of his severe disability and the depression that set in soon after the accident. The book has proved to be a great inspiration, and not only for those who are severely disabled – it also helps us to put our own problems into perspective.

As Apuu, Victor and many others in similar circumstances have shown, it is possible to overcome even the most severe disability and use it to inspire others. Both these young men have demonstrated how you can turn a negative experience into a positive one for yourself and others. They have shown that you can cherish the life that you have and be an important part of the lives of others, that you are needed here on Earth and have a role to play.

As for yourself, join every activity that you can. You too can make a difference to others who, when they see you upbeat and positive, will say: 'If he or she can still smile then I can overcome my small problems.' Whenever I meet a disabled person who has a smile – and most do – it is a humbling and powerful lesson to me and I know that most people react in the same way. You can show us the way!

All these situations and experiences can create a long list of negative emotions and attitudes, including:

- Hate
- Anger
- Bitterness
- Fear
- Distrust
- Despondency

- Guilt
- Jealousy

These emotions in turn create enormous negative thought forms for us to carry around which become a heavy load. They deplete our energy and prevent us from finding personal happiness and joy. They act as mind traps on our path forward, inhibiting us from gaining the best from life. But we do have a choice. We can either succumb to them or, like Apuu and Victor, we can overcome them.

- Do you want to be the victim or the victor of your own negative thoughts?
- Do you really want to suffer from your own negativity or grow and gain from the experience?

Turning the Negative into Positive

As we have seen, we can be the victim of not only our negative experiences but also their aftermath – our own emotions. Let's now look at ways in which you can take control and, like the young man in the wheelchair, be a victor. Use your experience to gain from life. You are the only one who can let go and clear away the negativity. You may not be able to forget the experiences that you have had, but you can change the way you think about life and people. You can change the way you think about yourself. You can change your attitude – you can see things from a positive rather than a negative perspective.

Gain from your experiences

Realise that you can grow from every experience, even a

negative one, and that your past has made you strong. Think back over your life and see all the positive advantages you have gained:

- Through giving and receiving love, no matter for how short a time, you have opened to the joy of sharing.
- Through accepting that others may be weaker and less evolved, you have learnt tolerance and understanding.
- Through your pain you have learnt empathy and compassion for others.
- Through facing death you have learnt to value life.

Sweep away negative thought forms

Part of my healing process is to sweep away the negative thought forms in my patient's aura. The thought forms feel sticky and heavy to the touch and I get different responses depending on how dense the negativity is that I am clearing away – I feel anything from a slight change in density to a full negative 'whoosh' through my entire body. Some of my students say that they feel hot and cold sensations in their fingers and hands when doing this. Sometimes I also see an inner picture of the event or the cause of the fear that has led to the creation of the thought form.

Aura clearing is a very simple process and one that you can use for clearing your own aura, as I will explain in the following exercise – I have already given you a mini-version of it earlier in the chapter. Even if you feel nothing with your hands you will get the benefit of feeling more peaceful and relaxed in yourself. Just trust that it's working. This process will sweep away the negative thought forms that you have created through worry and anxiety and I recommend doing it whenever you feel that you are getting stressed or worrying too much. It can help in the following ways:

- It will keep your aura energy free and flowing.
- It is a good remedy for headaches and 'muzziness' caused by tension or lack of good air.
- It relaxes and calms you down so it is great therapy to use before an important event or meeting. If you are nervous or apprehensive just do it for a few minutes.
- It can be used as a daily remedial exercise to keep yourself clear from blocks.

EXERCISE: 'COMBING' YOUR AURA

- Sit down and relax your shoulders.
- Breath in deeply and let your body go limp and soft.
- Imagine that your hands and fingers are a comb.
- 'Comb' through your aura from the outside towards your body, starting above your head and sweeping right down to your feet if you can reach them. If not, sweep to your knees and then flick away the energy. Try not to direct it to anyone – they won't thank you for your old negative energy. Throw it into a bowl of salt water, as salt absorbs negative energy, or visualise it burning in a violet flame.
- Do this for a few minutes – as the blocks start to clear you should start to feel lighter and more relaxed. As the energy around you becomes clearer your head should feel clearer too.

Release yourself from addiction

All addictions are a result of us giving away our power. If we are determined to regain that power – if we think we deserve that power back, if we think we are good enough – then we can do it. I know it's not easy to break the pattern of addiction – as I write I am in my second week of abstinence from refined sugar and chocolate, so I speak with feeling! One of the first things you need to establish is your trigger point – your motivation for saying to yourself 'enough is enough'. It may be your health, or the fact that you don't like being out of control, or that you won't be beaten by something outside of yourself. Or your addiction may be affecting those you love or your ability to work – whatever it is, find it and make it your reason for giving up.

How I gave up smoking

It can be hard to clear an addiction and as I said earlier in the chapter I am not qualified to help you if you have a serious addiction to hard drugs. However, if your addiction is to something like cigarettes, caffeine, Coke or chocolate you may like to try the following method based on my own experience of giving up smoking. It's essential that you are totally determined and clearly focused on what it is you want to give up and why. Your intention is the key here.

I used to be a heavy smoker in my twenties and the reason I gave up was vanity. I didn't think my slight but obvious smoker's cough did much for my chances of attracting Mr Wonderful. I also felt that smelly breath wasn't the greatest of sexual attractions. I read through the literature supplied by Anti-Smoking for Health (ASH), the organisation that helps smokers kick the habit. This was useful. ASH told me to find the reason for giving up and suggested that I cut down gradually day by day.

I also thought that I would try what is known as 'aversion therapy'. I decided to use visualisation to help me. I would visualise the cigarette together with something I abhorred and see the two as an item, in the hope that the loathsome part of the item would put me off all of it. So every time I thought about a cigarette (which was about thirty times a day) I made myself visualise a cigarette stubbed out in a bowl of porridge – my most hated food. I then pretended that I would have to eat the porridge. This helped tremendously and I managed to give up smoking. I haven't smoked since – and you won't be surprised to hear that I haven't eaten porridge again either. Here is a quick summary of the method I used for giving up cigarettes, which you can modify to apply to your own particular addiction.

EXERCISE: GIVING UP SMOKING

- Focus on your intention.
- Decide why you want to give up – for example, health, vanity, relationships, sociability and so on.
- Think of something you dislike intensely which you can visualise alongside a cigarette to put you off it.
- Set a target date. Make it realistic – but not too far in the future!
- Plan to decrease your consumption gradually day by day and tick off the days as you go.
- Avoid food and drinks that you associate with smoking.
- Try to use non-smoking areas of bars and restaurants to take away temptation.
- On the day you give up completely and the week after avoid all places where you habitually smoked. Move your desk or sitting room around so that there is a change in your environment.

Using Thoughts Positively

Once you are aware of the effect of your thoughts on yourself and others you can start to control them and use them to the best effect. Later we will look at many ways in which we can consciously make ourselves more positive but at this point let's see what we can do with our thoughts just by using our intent to help – both ourselves and other people.

Creating positive situations

We all have the benefit of free will and through this we can affect our experiences. By deliberately visualising the things that we need and seeing ourselves in happy circumstances we can help to make them happen. We will now look at how we can tap into the immense power of your mind. We will barely touch the surface of the deep power that we have within us but you will be amazed at what you can do with your intent and the positive vibrations of clear thoughts.

EXERCISE: BRING POSITIVE THINGS INTO YOUR LIFE

You can use this simple visualisation exercise to bring success, a loving partner, friendship and so on into your life – as long as your wish involves no harm to anyone, including yourself. Do be sure that you are calling into your life what you truly want, so rather than asking for 'money' ask for 'prosperity with joy', since money alone will not bring happiness.

- Decide on the situation you want to create or draw into your life. Don't be too specific with your wish. As you cannot always see the greater picture it's advisable to seek that which is the best for you. So if you want a partner or a new career don't ask for a specific person or job to be drawn to you but ask for the best there is for you. You never know, there might be a more suitable person or job just waiting for you around the corner.

- Find a quiet place where you will not be disturbed by the phone or other interruptions.
- Light a candle.
- Sit down and make yourself comfortable.
- Breathe in deeply four times and relax your shoulders.
- Look at the candle for a moment then close your eyes.
- Visualise the lit candle in front of you.
- Visualise the situation that you wish to create.
- See the situation and the candle merge into a flash of light.
- Now speak inside your head, saying what it is you wish to create. Don't use the word 'wish' but rather say: 'I create . . . in my life, if it will truly benefit me in all ways.' Say this four times. Make sure there is some benefit for others in your wish, for example: 'If I get this job I'll be able to support my family.' Never wish for anything that is detrimental to others. I use the phrase: 'Let it be for the greatest good of all.'
- Hold your hands to your heart and say: 'I create . . . in my life with love.'

You have now used your will, your mind and your heart to create your vision. There is great power in this potent combination of intention, contemplation and love.

Prayer and distance healing

For centuries humankind has recognised the benefits of prayer. Prayers consist of thoughts that are intended to benefit the receiver, whether this be God, individuals or groups of people needing help. Because God is all that is – the creator of each one of us and of our universe – all prayers addressed to God will help every one of us. Whatever your spiritual inclination you can use the power of your mind to help yourself and others by directing your thoughts purposefully and with good intentions to uplift and heal.

The following exercise is for sending positive vibrations to a person, a group of people or to the planet Earth. To assist you here is a symbol that you can use as a 'magnet' to draw the healing energies into your intentions. It will also help you with your visualisation – for me it acts like a zoom lens and brings into focus the person I am visualising for healing.

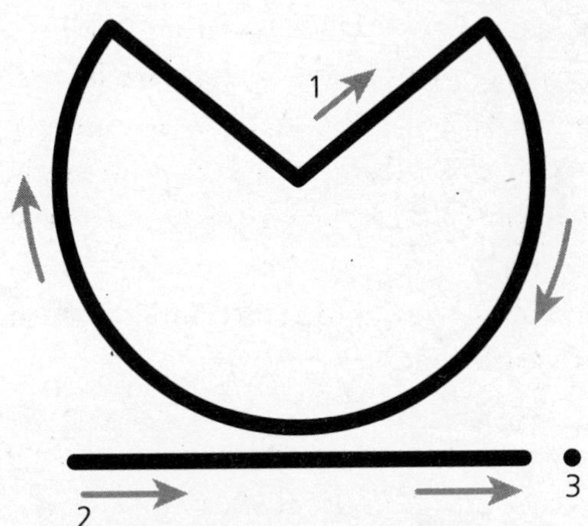

You can use this symbol to help you send out positive healing vibrations to people when they are not present.

Exercise: Directing Healing Thoughts

- Find a quiet place where you will not be disturbed.
- Make yourself completely at ease and comfortable. If you wish put on very quiet background music to absorb any outside noise.
- Burn aromatherapy oils like lavender that will help you relax, or incense if you prefer.
- Light a candle with the intention of lighting up the world.
- Have with you photographs or the names of those who you wish to help.
- Close your eyes and breathe in deeply, feeling your body relaxing more and more deeply with each breath.
- Try to visualise a candle with a huge flame. If you can't visualise it then just know that the flame is there. This flame represents the healing powers of light.
- Now send beams of love to the flame. Feel your intention to love.
- Trace the distance healing symbol in the air with your dominant hand or on the photograph if you have one, or even visualise the symbol.
- See the people you want to heal one by one step into the flame.
- See them happy and well and infused with the light. You will only need to hold the image for a few seconds.
- Now see animals, trees, oceans and anything that you want to heal in the environment in the candle flame.
- See the entire planet Earth spinning in the healing light.
- Finally, see yourself in the flame and let yourself be healed by it.

A QUICK VERSION

When you have a few spare moments – while waiting for that train or stuck in the traffic jam – you can do a shorter version of the exercise. You can use a photograph for this as well.

- Cup your hands and imagine that the person you want to heal is in your hands.
- Envisage the distance healing symbol or, if you can, trace it in your palm.
- Feel the energies of love and compassion flow into the person that you have in your hand.

Seeing things from a positive perspective

Being positive is an attitude of mind. It is about seeing life from a different perspective, for example:

- Seeing the glass as half full rather than half empty.
- Seeing the obstacles in your life as challenges to overcome.
- Seeing difficulties as opportunities to grow and develop yourself and your character.
- Seeing life as a journey of opportunity rather than a trial.
- Seeing the good in people rather than the bad.
- Seeing the good in yourself rather than the bad.
- Seeing your experiences as assets to use for the future.
- Seeing the sunshine rather than the gloom.
- Seeing the good points of even the gloom.
- Seeing the upside of things, whenever you can.
- Seeing the best in the present moment and not dwelling on the past.

Speaking with a positive voice

Adopting this perspective will change you from a negative thinker to a positive one. One way in which you can help yourself change the way you think is through positive declarations or affirmations. Our voice is a powerful tool to help us move towards the positive. We can say things that are positive and the sound of our voice will send high vibrations throughout our entire being. We will be doubly affected as we hear ourselves pronouncing upbeat and encouraging views.

By making positive declarations we will also break the habit of being negative. We will start a new habit – being positive. What we are doing is really a form of self-brainwashing and we need to repeat our affirmations many times in order to break our old habits. So say them out loud with meaning and with determined intention. You will need to think up your own affirmations based on your own requirements but here are some examples for you to get the idea:

- I am confident and fearless.
- I am able to overcome my anxieties.
- I respect myself.
- I can do it.
- I can achieve it.
- I call prosperity and abundance to me.
- I am lucky.
- I am fortunate.
- I am successful.
- I am loved.

Connecting to Positive Energy Streams

We are surrounded by streams of energy. Some of these are potentially harmful, as we shall see when we look at the emissions of overhead electricity cables and microwave pylons. But many of them are positive. Here we will look at how we can connect to, and take advantage of, these positive energy sources. First let's look at the positive energy created by people.

Connect to positive people

You can connect to the energy created by people whom you feel have the qualities and energy levels that you would like for yourself. If they are strong they will be constantly emitting beneficial forces and just by thinking of them you can tap into the stream of positive energy that they exude. In the past we have done this through worship. When people have thought of and prayed to Jesus, the Buddha, Vishnu or any other spiritual figure they have connected to that figure's essence or the energy it has emitted. The worshipper feels uplifted by the connection.

Football fans do the same thing with their heroes and pop fans do it to their idols. Just by thinking of them they feel good. Their idols stand for something that they want – prestige, skill, success, confidence and so on.

We can do this to attract all the positive energy forces of others, such as strength, courage, love and respect. If you want to feel stronger, think of someone you respect who has strength and see a beam of light from them coming to you. Don't forget to thank them for it!

Connect to the healing energies of nature

Nature is a great source of strong and wholesome energy! The sea, rocks and mountains, flowers, trees, animals, rivers and so on all give off a stream of good energy. This is why we feel so good after a weekend in the country, a stroll through a park, or a trip to the seaside. Plants also help us by oxygenating the air so they are doubly beneficial. So take any opportunity you can to take a walk in the countryside or your local park. Fill your home with plants. A trip to the sea will bring extra benefits as the salt in the ocean will attract and clear the negativity around you.

Connect to universal energies

Apart from the positive vibes that we get from nature there is another important source of powerful energy that we can tap into. This is the universal energy that is available to everyone. The creator of the universe used extremely powerful vibrations to make the whole thing happen – the Big Bang – and this energy is available for us to use too.

The highest vibration and the strongest power for good is universal love. I personally like to add the energies of compassion too as these are soft and warm and give us empathy with all living beings. These are the energies that I use for healing. I connect with them then direct them to the person who needs healing. This is easy enough actually – all I need is the intention and it will happen, as it will if you also choose to connect.

At the end of this chapter I have written a short meditation in which we connect with the light and the energies of love and compassion. In the meantime, an exercise using a healing symbol that I have been given will automatically connect you with those energies and attract them to you. The symbol invokes the energy and then you can decide whether to use it for yourself or direct it to others, or both. Here it is:

The healing symbol can be used to invoke the universal energies of love and compassion.

Exercise: Attracting Positive Energy with the Healing Symbol

- Trace the symbol in the air in front of you three times, working from right to left and ending up with the dot.
- Place your hand on your body. Just let the energies flow through your hand and into your body. Place your hand wherever you are hurting. If are worried or anxious then place it on your chest below your throat. This will help you to release your anxieties. If you have any strong fear or butterflies in your stomach

place your hand on your solar plexus. Or if you want to connect to the wonderful energies of love, place your hand over your heart in the middle of your chest.

Other Ways to Revitalise Your Energy

We will now look at some other ways in which you can influence the energy levels of your body. All of these activities will help you to raise your energy.

Energy healing

I have mentioned how you can personally connect to the power of universal energy and use this to uplift your energy levels. Reiki therapists and other natural energy healers access this energy source and can channel it through for you. Energy healing is a wonderful way to clear negativity caused by past experiences and it will help you to re-generate your energy flow, to relax, and to heal mental, emotional and physical disorders. My healing organisation, Hearts and Hands, gives workshops and healing sessions; for further information contact us directly or through our website (see contact details on page 285).

Colour therapy

One of the most potent ways for us to clear negative energy from ourselves is to lift our energy. We can use colour very effectively for this because every colour has a different vibration. You can change your mood, lift your spirits and re-energise yourself by choosing colours for your clothes and decor that work for you.

Generally, the brighter and more vibrant the colour the more uplifting it will be. Yellow is the colour I would naturally choose for my home to create the feeling of sunlight and joy. Lavender is peaceful and relaxing. Pink is the colour of the heart, so if you need to improve your love life or you need help healing a broken heart then wear pink.

Wear blue, the colour of communication, if you are having trouble with expressing your feelings. Blue is also healing, as is green. To help connect with your imagination and intuition wear the spiritual colour purple. Wear white if you want to clear something and let it go – white suggests purity and is good for clearing and also has spiritual resonance. Red is a power colour and will give you strength. Orange is energising.

Browns, greys and black are not likely to boost your energies although you may like the slimming effect of black and it seems to be every woman's choice for evening wear! Take a look at the colours that you have around you and that you wear and see if you can't lift yourself up by a change. Go lighter and brighter.

The effects of the vibrations of colour have been recognised by healers and many therapists have now developed various ways to magnify these effects with apparatus and the use of modern technology. There is a newly developed system that utilises lasers, colour and gemstones to create a powerful healing tool. By sending laser beams of light through the appropriate gem and colour, the system magnifies their healing power.

This system can not only lift your energies but also often cure many diseases and ailments – there has been particular success with asthma and psoriasis (for more details of gemstone therapy see Further Reading, page 282).

Electromagnetic therapy

There are a number of devices on the market that actually employ electromagnetic fields to balance and clear the energy system, and in recent years these have become well established and affordable. More detailed information on electromagnetic therapies and other equipment using modern technology can be found in *Virtual Medicine* by Dr Keith Scott-Mumby (see Further Reading, page 283).

Aromatherapy oils

Some aromatherapy oils are particularly beneficial for raising your energies. You can use these oils in the bath, in burners or in a massage-oil base. The following oils will uplift spirits, energise and help relieve depression:

- Bergamot
- Clary sage
- Geranium
- Lemon
- Orange
- Patchouli
- Peppermint
- Rose
- Sandalwood
- Ylang ylang

Flower essences

Flower essences are created from the flowers of plants, bushes and trees. The flower is picked when it is mature and preserved in mineral water. The energy of the plant with its unique qualities is then available for treating personality and emotional problems. The different vibration frequencies emitted by plants have been found to have different effects on our emotional, spiritual and mental bodies. They work on our characteristics, attitudes and behaviour.

The groundbreaker in this form of therapy was Edward Bach, who developed a range of flower essences that are now widely available through all leading chemists and natural health shops. There are thirty-eight different Bach Flower Remedies for balancing and correcting many emotional states, and it would be worth your while to look at the full range some time. Other essences have been developed using plants from different parts of the world, and you are probably best advised to use your local products as they will suit local conditions.

If you can't decide which remedy most suits your personal requirements then close your eyes and hold your hands over the selection and let your senses lead you to the one you need. The ones I have suggested here are particularly good for raising you out of negativity and giving your spirits a lift:

- **Elm** For being overwhelmed by responsibility.
- **Gentian** For despondency.
- **Gorse** For pessimism.
- **Mustard** For sadness and feeling miserable for no obvious reason.
- **Oak** For strength.
- **Olive** For fatigue, loss of energy.
- **Sweet chestnut** For dejection.
- **Wild rose** For apathy.

Massage

All massage treatments will relax your muscles and help to clear the internal physical blocks that stop natural energy flow. A variety of forms of massage is now readily available and most towns will have full-time masseurs in health centres and beauty salons. Which type of massage you use is entirely a matter of personal preference. I prefer the gentler types and my choice is a medium-pressure aromatherapy massage. For a truly uplifting and awakening experience you would ask your therapist to blend particular oils for this purpose (see above). Shiatsu (which is done through your clothes) and acupressure are stronger forms of massage that act on the pressure points and meridians in a similar way to acupuncture.

Acupuncture

This ancient therapy comes from the East but has made a great impression everywhere in the past few years. The practitioner will insert fine needles (they don't hurt, by the way) into the surface of the skin at certain key 'pressure points' to clear energy blocks and open up the meridians, the energy lines that run through and around our body. Acupuncture has a similar effect to energy sweeping and reflexology.

Reflexology

A reflexologist uses his or her hands or a crystal to stimulate pressure points on the patient's feet that correspond to areas of the body. By clearing the crystals that develop at these points, the reflexologist clears the energy flow through the meridians to the corresponding areas. This is an extremely pleasant form of healing if you like having your feet touched. By massaging the pressure points in the feet reflexology can clear your energy flow and help to cure you of any energy imbalances.

Chiropractic balancing

Most people face occupational hazards of one kind or another and many of us now spend hours in front of a computer screen. Every six months I visit a chiropractor for an all-over check-up and balancing session. I find this helps clear any potential problems and relieves accumulated tension, particularly in my shoulders and back. Massage will clear small problems and help relax muscles, but a chiropractor can put bones and muscles back into place and this in itself will clear many of our blockages. My own chiropractor combines a number of therapeutic modes to create an incredible healing experience.

Sports

All sporting activities will raise your energy, although you may feel exhausted in the short term. There are several benefits from sport and any other method of getting fit. First, it takes your focus away from your daily problems and anxieties and relieves tension. Second, the exercise will make the blood circulate throughout your body, taking oxygen to all your vital parts and keeping the heart and lungs healthy. Third, as well as oxygenating the blood, exercise causes the brain to produce endorphins – or 'happy vibes' – that immediately give you a lift. Finally, when you are physically fit you will have a better metabolism that will help your body to be more efficient in its physical transformation of your food and drink into energy. Remember to start gently if you are unused to vigorous physical activity of this sort.

Yoga

Yoga deserves a special mention as it is extremely therapeutic and works on body, mind and spirit. Through the postures of yoga you will release all tension, blocks and stress not only physically but also in your energy field. If done properly and guided by a good teacher, yoga is also a moving form of meditation that helps you to relax your entire being and get in touch with your inner self.

Music

We all respond to different types of music, but find the one that gives you a positive lift and allow yourself to be absorbed by it. Turn up the volume and let rip. Whether it be *The Planets* suite by Holst or head-banging rock, just go with it. It is one of the quickest ways to raise your spirits that I know.

Dance

Another quick pick-me-up is having a dance. I personally love modern dancing as it allows you to do just what you feel. Go with the flow. I'm not too keen on ballroom dancing or any choreographed movement – even the Macarana is much too controlling for my unfettered energy! Which is also another way of saying I can never remember the steps – the same problem I have with aerobics. If you don't want to go so far as to boogie down at the local club on a Friday night then just use your kitchen as a dance floor, put on your favourite CD and off you go.

Good food

Of course all food will supply us with energy, but we are well advised to avoid food that contains any form of additive. Processed foods and ingredients – like white rice, white sugar and white flour – don't give us the same energy value as less refined products. Eat organic and fresh vegetables, fruits and meat whenever you can. I have given a further detailed overview of the effects of different food in Chapter 4.

Drink

There are a number of herbal teas that you may find helpful. I like peppermint tea as it is very refreshing and not as sweet as some herbal teas, and you may like to try Japanese green tea as this is very healthy and has no additives to slow you down.

Supplements

There are many supplements on the market now that are advertised as energy enhancers and I suggest you get advice about them at your local health food shop or pharmacy. I use Coenzyme Q10 and I find it works every time. It comes in different dosages and I will only use the highest dosage if I have to work all day and all evening too, otherwise it will stop me sleeping at night. It really is most effective. Ginseng is an all-round health enhancer, and another favourite of mine is echinacea, which I take when there are colds and flu about and I want my immune system to have an extra boost.

Entertainment and laughter

There is nothing as enhancing and uplifting as a good laugh. So if you want to be inspired and elevated gravitate towards comedies and non-violent films. I love the films that come out for children – they are often adults' movies in disguise!

So there are many ways in which we can raise our energies and uplift our spirits. Let's lastly look at creating a space in our home where we can relax and completely chill out, a place where we can release the stresses of our day.

A Healing Space

Wherever you live it is a great idea to have some space that you allocate for relaxation and healing. Create a place in your home that will trigger the idea of relaxation as soon as you sit down, a place where you can clear yourself of the day's troubles. It can be a chair by a window in your bedroom, or a spare room that you can adopt and adapt for yourself. It can be a spot in your garden where you create a sanctuary, surrounding yourself with your favourite flowers and shrubs. A friend of mine has taken over the summer house in her garden.

Another way to make the space and time sacred is to burn oils or incense and light a candle as a symbol to the universe that you are calming down and healing at this time. In my special place I have pictures of spiritual masters, crystals, photos and tokens that have memories of special moments. I also keep a list of the people who need healing. Sometimes I like to have my quiet time in the bath – then I burn candles and put aromatherapy oil in the bath to help me relax and meditate.

Exercise: Filling Yourself with Light

Meditation is an excellent way for you to relax and to find that quiet place inside yourself. Guided meditation enables you to still yourself mentally, physically and spiritually by visualising and focusing on a given subject. This is a simple meditation and visualisation that you can do to help you to let go of your worries and bring yourself into a positive and light state. As with all the meditations we will be doing throughout this book you can memorise it, record it on a cassette, ask a friend to read it to you, or order the CD from Hearts and Hands (see page 285).

- Find a quiet and serene place – such as your personal healing space – for your meditation.
- Sit or lie down as comfortably as you can. If you can sit cross-legged then that is fine, but the most important factor is that you are comfortable so that you can concentrate on the meditation.
- Once you are comfortable, close your eyes and breathe in deeply a few times. Take air right into the recesses of your lungs, deep down where we keep our anxieties.
- Let your shoulders drop and allow your entire body to go soft.
- Now we will use our imagination. See yourself on a glorious beach, completely empty apart from you. You are paddling in the shallow water. The Sun is shining on your back and keeping you gently warm.
- Your feet are in the cool water of the sea – feel your

toes digging into the soft sand. Feel a strong connection with the beach and the sea. Sense the sound of the waves and the smell of seaweed and the salty aroma of the sea.

- Imagine a white light appearing that envelops your feet. As it surrounds your feet, feel them relax.
- See this light move up your body, concentrating in turn on your feet, legs, thighs, back, shoulders, arms, neck and head.
- Move your focus down your face, letting the light clear away any tension and letting go of the care lines and furrows on your brow. Let your frown fly away. Feel your face covered in white light.
- Think of your throat and feel the tendons in your neck relax. The light is loosening any tightness caused by fear of speaking or by sickness and ill health.
- Move the light on down your oesophagus to your lungs and then down to your stomach, and feel your insides become soft as you let go of any anger that you may be holding there. Keep on relaxing.
- Think of your sexual organs and sense them becoming relaxed, fill them with light and let go of all tension. Think of your liver, your spleen and your kidneys. See them as healthy and filled with light.
- Sense your entire body as filled and surrounded with light and take a few moments to feel the strength this gives you.
- Now sit down in the sea and feel the waves caressing your body, cleansing you with the cool salt water. Imagine that all your negativity is being washed away by the gentle motion of the lapping water.
- Splash the water all over your body and see yourself clearing away all negative thought forms.
- Roll in the surf and let the salt water clear your entire body.

- Now stand up strong and walk with great strides down the beach as you step forward in your life, with energy, with courage and with determination.
- See this clear and magnificent beach ahead of you as your life and the future. Now you are cleansed you can repel any negative thought or action that comes from any source. You are so light and confident that you will only attract light and uplifting experiences from now on.
- Close your eyes and turn your face to the Sun. Know that you are attracting the powerful light of the Sun to you now. Feel the Sun's energy fill your entire being. Bask in its light and power.
- Visualise yourself overcoming all the obstacles and challenges in your life with this power of light. Imagine it issuing from you in great rays. See yourself as a being of great power, as a being of pure light. Nothing can touch you, nobody can have dominance over you, for you are invincible.
- Spend a few moments glorying in this power and strength. See your troubles obliterated by the light you shed on all.
- Slowly come back from the sea and into the room where you are sitting, bringing your light and strength with you.

I suggest you do this visualisation regularly every few days or whenever you are depressed or stressed. If you do it in the mornings it will help you be calm and ready for the day ahead and you will find that stressful events will have less impact on you. In the evenings it will calm you down and take away the stresses of the day. Before going to bed it will help you to sleep.

* * *

We have looked at the way that our own negative thoughts and attitudes can affect our health and well-being. In the following chapter we are going to see how we can be affected by the negativity of other people and how we can protect and clear ourselves from its effects.

3

Other People's Negativity

Whether we like it or not we are surrounded by negativity. In this chapter we shall first look at how those around us – our family and work colleagues, other people in general – can affect our energy unconsciously and consciously. Later on I will give you some help with protection and cleansing.

The Effects of Group Energy

Unless we have chosen the life of a hermit we will come into contact with other people in our daily lives and therefore be affected by their thoughts and behaviour. First I am going to look at the problem of what I call 'passive negativity'. This is the form of negativity that is created by the thoughts, attitudes and behaviour of people who are *not* intending to harm us or disturb us, but who are carrying around their problems and so will cause a reaction in our own emotions and feelings if we come into contact with them.

When your energy field comes close to another person's you absorb some of the energies of that person. If they are happy and cheerful this can give you a lift, but if they are depressed and downcast you will be affected by the negativity in their aura – it will move across into your own. The more sensitive you are the more other people will affect you. You will also be affected if you are feeling weak and vulnerable. The stronger you are the less likely you are to be affected. However, most of us will be affected by large groups.

Let's look at what happens when we travel somewhere. Every time we leave our homes and travel on public transport – by bus, train or plane – we are surrounded by people whose minds are working away creating thoughts – creating energy. I find I am particularly affected when flying, when we are cooped up in a small space for a considerable time with strangers.

I believe this is the reason that travelling can be so tiring. We never know who we are sitting next to on a plane and we don't know what energies we are exposed to as we munch through our in-flight meal. So at the end of this chapter I have included several techniques that you can use to protect yourself from these unknown energies; I advise you to make sure that you do this before you set off on your travels.

Some of you will, of course, be more sensitive than others. I knew of a healer who began to feel pain from the people around her once she started to open up to her new powers. Life became impossible for her until she learnt to shut herself down a little and to open up only when she needed to connect with her patients. As I have mentioned, I feel the emotions of others and this has been a great asset for healing but can be a downright problem in a crowd. I have also now learnt to separate myself from those around me, which you can do without being unfriendly but just by holding your space for yourself.

You may work with large groups of people so you will also need to protect yourself and put up some form of defence around you. Once you are aware of the effects that groups can have upon you, your intention to be separate and detached will take you ninety per cent of the way there.

Check your own reactions over the next few days. Monitor how you are in a group. How do you feel when you walk into a room full of people? Use the protection processes at the end of the chapter and then see if there are any changes. You will be amazed how effective even the simplest methods can be.

Group Thought Forms

We have looked at how we as individuals create 'thought forms' with our thoughts, emotions and attitudes. Now we will look at how groups of people can also create thought forms in the same way. If enough people think the same way and have the same thoughts constantly the energy of their thoughts combines to create a 'group thought form'.

The vibration of the group thoughts act like a magnet – like attracts like – and the mass of energy that results will obviously have more power (either positive or negative) than the thought form of an individual.

Religions and miracles

Positive group thought forms can arise among religious believers and spiritual followings. For example, as Christianity grew so did the energy connected with Jesus – a group thought form generated by the love and dedication that thousands of people felt for Him. When an individual taps into this positive energy he or she can feel the love of the thousands of others who think and feel the same way. The love and prayers sent to, and focused on, Jesus over two millennia have become an almost tangible thing – an energy form so strong that individuals can be immensely affected just by thinking of it.

Miracles can happen when people attract this powerful positive energy, either by concentrating on a much-worshipped spiritual figure such as Jesus or by visiting a place where immense positive group energies have amassed.

One such place is Lourdes, the famous pilgrimage site in southern France where, about 150 years ago, a young woman called Bernadette had visions of the Virgin Mary. A sacred spring is said to have sprung up, and since then many thousands of pilgrims have gone to Lourdes to worship at the site of the visions and to be cured by the waters of the spring. They have taken with them their devotion to Mary and Jesus, and the energy of their thoughts has amassed to create a place of great energy and power.

Group energy of nations

Another type of group thought form is that created by nations. In the past this type of thought form was strong and specific. For an example, let's look at Japan, a country that deliberately kept itself quite isolated from the rest of the world and was therefore not influenced by other cultures. Japan experienced very little interference from other countries right up to the 20th century and was able to develop its own culture unaffected by the thoughts and observations of others. The outcome of this was that the Japanese character was unique and clearly defined – there were clear and distinctive characteristics and ways of behaving that could be found in almost all its citizens.

Many of these traits and customs can still be seen today. The Japanese are very polite and formally deferential, still bowing to those they consider above them either at work or socially. They are also extremely tidy – their gardens are immaculate. The most noticeable characteristic, though, is the way individual thoughts and feelings often firmly take second place to those of the group.

When I visited Japan six years ago I thought that the people were extremely controlled – they suppress any outward show of personal emotion most of the time. They are hard-working and perfectionists – their trains run like clockwork to an impressively accurate timetable – on the rare occasions a train is late each member of the train staff will apologise to every passenger in person. They are also very considerate of their neighbours, as they have to live so closely together that they have found thoughtfulness for those around them to be essential for a harmonious existence.

In the past, this deference to the group has shown itself as fierce nationalism and, as we know, many Japanese were prepared to give their lives for their country, considering it a great honour to make this sacrifice.

Of course, with modern technologies Japan is now fully open to the rest of the world and many of the distinctive characteristics and thinking habits of its people are likely to be dissipated. However, individuals still remain strongly affected by the energy of the group and Japan's national group thought form will continue to exist for some considerable time.

The energy of group thought forms like these can have a positive or negative impact upon us. Let's look at just some of the many instances of how we can be affected by group energy.

Group sorrow

One of the most powerful experiences I have had of group energy was at the time of Princess Diana's death in 1997. I was amazed at the way the nation – and many overseas countries too – were so profoundly affected. I understood that Diana was an icon and as such represented youth, beauty and a lifestyle that many would aspire to. However, I didn't have any particularly strong feelings about her and although I felt sympathy for her, I certainly wasn't a devoted fan of hers. Nevertheless, I found myself deeply moved and shocked by her death, and for days I had a pain in my heart centre – this is the energy point in the centre of the chest where we feel the strong emotions of love. I felt as though I had lost someone really close to me.

It took me a while to realise that I was sensing the feelings of the nation. So many people were so deeply affected by sadness that the energy of sorrow had become contagious and had swept from one person's aura to another like a great stream, until the atmosphere around us all was filled with the grief. Eventually the country had become as one and people who would not normally have cried over the loss of a public figure were seen to be weeping openly. It was as if the heart centre of the entire nation was hurt and we as a group were feeling and grieving as one being. I have spoken of this to others since and they have recognised that they too were affected by the sorrowful mood of the public.

Group power

We can also be uplifted and inspired by large groups. If you have ever been to a rock concert or the Last Night of the Proms you will have felt the great surge of elation that comes from listening to music that is powerfully charged. If one was listening to the same music but sitting alone either at home or even in an empty concert hall the effects would be nowhere near the same.

A similar effect is felt in a sports stadium filled with fans supporting a single contestant or a team. We can get completely carried away by the atmosphere. Our excitement adds to that of the rest of the fans and the atmosphere can become tangible, almost electric.

Now here is something to think about: the energy created by the group is greater than the sum of the energy produced by the individuals in the group. The energy becomes magnified as it comes together – the vibration rises as more and more energy unites. There is a mathematical formula for this but you now know that such formulae are not my strong point. But it means that if ten people are thinking the same thing, the power of their thought energy is multiplied by itself, generating the same amount of power as if 100 people were individually creating the same thought. This amazing reaction seems to be most effective when the people are all in the same place. Maybe this is because then they are all completely in harmony and focused.

Hearts and Hands, my healing organisation, works on

this principle of magnified group healing power at its Peace Festivals. These are gatherings held throughout the world with the express intention of bringing together as many people as possible. In this way we can create an amazing amount of positive thought energy to send healing to humanity and the planet. If there is a festival being held near you, please come as every single person makes a huge difference in the raising of the group vibration, not only of those at the festival but of everyone in the world.

Someone once told me that if we brought 144,000 people together we could change the energy of the entire planet Earth and every living being. I like a challenge and this is my aim – to gather that many of us together and make an impact on world energy vibrations. With the higher vibrations come the emotions of love, and I am in no doubt that with love we shall have peace.

Group dominance

When people get together their energies combine and create a new life form. The Native Americans have always recognised this and call this life form a *manitou*. The group creates its own consciousness and will and there is always the danger that once we become part of this new consciousness we may lose some of our own individual power and will. We often see how an individual will behave totally differently when part of a group. To start with we are far more controllable once we align ourselves with this new group consciousness and our own will is weakened. We can be more easily manipulated by powerful leaders who wish to impose their will upon us.

In some cases this can be a very positive experience, for example, the joy that we can feel at a concert or listening to an uplifting and inspirational speech. I can remember weeping with the emotions of compassion and love when Bob Geldof, who organised the Live Aid concerts in the 1980s, spoke of the suffering of the people of Ethiopia. I was at home watching this event on television, and it must have been so much more moving live. In the Second World War, Winston Churchill lifted the entire British nation with his speeches and inspired people to find levels of courage, strength and dedication that they could never have achieved alone.

However, giving away our power to the group can also have negative and even disastrous results. What happens in war, when men leave their normal lives to become part of an army, is a common example. It has also been seen recently in the mass suicides of members of religious cults who were completely dominated by a powerful leader. Such figures can use their powerful charisma to lead their vulnerable followers to perform acts which, as individuals, they would never contemplate and which are detrimental to their individual well-being.

It is worth bearing in mind that whenever you are in a group, no matter how benign it may seem, and no matter how small, remember to hold on to your own values at all times. Keep a grip on your own principles and beliefs and don't be completely overwhelmed by the emotions of the group. Hitler would have had far less effect on the people of Germany if they had kept to their own values and not given themselves over to the power of his dominance.

Group menace

The dreadful deeds perpetrated by mobs have left scars on the history of humanity. On television recently I watched a community in Indonesia being attacked and its homes plundered by a screaming mob of neighbours. These people had lived side by side for years as friends and had helped each other through their difficult times. It was dreadful to see them change into a mob baying for blood. What did they feel afterwards when peace was restored – what guilt are they going to live with?

We have all seen the effects of riots and mobs – on the television news if not as eyewitnesses. I always feel sick in my stomach when I see people running out of control – not because they are beyond the control of the authorities but because they are beyond their *own* control. Most of the worst injustices and most dreadful massacres of the world have been perpetrated by mobs who have been incited to violence and rage by a manipulative leader or leaders.

Fanaticism is created when one individual generates a wholly negative group thought form. This is a group mindset and belief system in which the focus on a particular ideal or goal – which may initially be positive – becomes so intense that all perspective is lost, together with tolerance and compassion towards those who do not share the ideal. The terrible deeds of 11 September, 2001, and the grief and suffering that this caused for so many, sprang directly from the fanaticism incited by just one charismatic individual. We have all now seen the results of a fanatical group consciousness and what can happen when the normal values of the individuals who make up a group are overshadowed and obliterated.

Resisting negative group energy

So what can we do about this? Most mob outrages are committed far away. They are things we watch on television. They are not happening here, among our friends and family. Or are they? You may be surprised how these group actions are being mirrored right under your nose. And you *can* do something and make a difference.

Most importantly, don't allow yourself to be caught up by the wishes and attitudes of others. At work, even in an office, you will find that there are always some people who have a lot to say for themselves, who want others to follow their line of thinking. They can coerce you into taking their side in debates and may even inspire you to turn against others, notwithstanding your better judgement. Gossip and cliques in an office have the potential to spread negativity.

Have you ever kept quiet when a group has started to talk about someone, rather than spoken up for them? Have you ever joined in gossip and spoken detrimentally about someone you actually like? Have you become part of an office vendetta? Have you found yourself thinking badly of someone just because of hearsay? Have you ever let someone else take the blame because you have been encouraged to do so by a group of friends? We have all allowed ourselves to be swayed by a group at some time in our lives – just remember the harm it can do and how guilty we feel about it afterwards.

What happens in a small way in an office or workplace reflects what is going on in the world at large. By setting your own standards and sticking to them you will have an impact not only on those around you but also on people throughout the world. The 'ripple effect' spreads far wider than you can imagine. Remember that the energy of your thoughts is a continuous stream that will affect all who connect to it. We create these streams of energy with everything we do and say, so by holding your position, by standing up for the persecuted – even in the office – you are generating strong and positive energy for the good of all humanity – including yourself.

The Energy of Individuals

Now we will see what effect individuals can have on our energy. We will look at the negativity that can come from our family, friends and others, how their behaviour and attitudes affect us – and how we react to them.

Your family

Let's start by looking at the type of energy that you may come across in the home. If you share your life with someone who doesn't have the same outlook as you then you will be affected by them. If they are downbeat and negative this will make you feel depressed, low or even angry. If they are positive and upbeat then they will most likely uplift you as well.

First we'll look at the positive effects of living and sharing your life with people who are themselves light and positive. To give you an idea of the effects that the family can have on us I will share with you the effect on me of some of my own family members.

The first person to come to mind is my husband's daughter. She is a bright and sunny young woman who has an extremely uplifting and positive effect when she visits or even calls on the phone. She affects my husband in the same way – she is a joy to be with. We may not always agree with everything she says, but that's not the issue here – it is her attitude and positivity that affects us all. She may feel low from time to time like we all do but it is never for long and her optimistic attitude to everything is marvellously refreshing. She knows her own mind so doesn't drain us with dithering – we will talk more about this later – and has a clear view on what pleases her.

My mother also has an uplifting effect upon me. She is also a very determined and strong character and very, very loving. She also always holds her line and knows what she wants. This made my upbringing very easy – any rules she set stayed set, a good situation because clear boundaries are important for a child. She has a great attitude towards me and has let me be my own person and make my own decisions without trying to impress her views upon me. She has loved me unconditionally and never expects anything in return.

Of course, this means I feel free to give to her in every way as I know I won't be smothered. So many mothers think that loving means smothering. The greatest gift we can give our children is the ability to make their own way with guidance and love but without dominance. This way she has made me feel strong and able to find my own path in life.

My husband is another strong character. He is successful in his career and exudes confidence. He is very loving to me but because of our work we are apart quite a lot. Again he doesn't smother me or dominate me but offers ongoing support. He is well grounded and balanced and doesn't need to score points from me to feel good in himself. His strength, tolerance and cool attitude to life make me feel safe and protected and unthreatened in any way. This allows me to grow and be myself.

As you can see I am exceptionally blessed with those near to me, and I have a host of other family members and friends who are equally positive and strong. However, we are not all surrounded by such uplifting energies. The following exercise will help you to understand why on some days you feel uplifted and energised and on others you feel drained. For a great deal of the time you will be reacting to the people around you. If you can identify who boosts you and who brings you down you will be able to neutralise and protect yourself from negative experiences and to recognise and maximise positive ones.

Exercise: Take an Energy Check

- Write a list of all the people with whom you spend a good proportion of your time – your closest family members, friends and work colleagues. Include anyone else in your life who influences you or otherwise has an impact upon you.
- Write down the main characteristics of each person.
- Write down the effects each person has on you, both positive and negative. What sort of emotional reaction do they prompt in you? What behaviour traits do they bring out in you? Do you behave differently with different people? Do you get irritated by some people? Do you get angry with others?

Once you have identified the good points in your family, friends and colleagues then make sure you tell them. It's amazing how people flourish when they are honestly applauded or praised in any way and you will find that they will optimise their good points once you have acknowledged them. People generally want to please and they definitely want to be loved. If you can give them some encouragement you will draw the best from them.

Dealing with Difficult Personality Traits

I am now going to identify some of the characteristics, attitudes and behaviour patterns you may find in the people you know. I will explain their positive and negative effects and the reactions that they may draw from you. Bear in mind that these characteristics are often interrelated, for example habitual stubbornness may be a manifestation of either egotism or an underlying fearfulness.

Once you know what you are up against you can start to work on how to deal with it. By handling certain people in a different way, they have a less negative affect upon you. They may even change their behaviour and treat you differently too. Try to be empathic and see things from the other person's viewpoint – this can sometimes diffuse our initial negative reactions. Remember also always to look for the best in everybody – finding the best will bring out the best.

Anger

When someone is angry with themselves they tend to take it out on everyone around them. This means they can be aggressive and difficult. Teenagers are often angry because they are seeking their way in the world and, quite understandably, finding it hard and confusing. They have a lot to assimilate and are often strongly influenced by peer pressure – which will very likely be at odds with the opinion of authority or their parents. A person who is angry is often overwhelmed by life and feels unable to cope. This makes them frustrated, which can lead to anger with themselves for failing in some way.

Anger can also be a reaction to unfair treatment or

abuse in childhood. Deep inner anger is different from the quick flash most of us all feel when crossed. Here I am talking about the simmering anger that can flare suddenly and often for little or no apparent reason. Men who abuse their wives are normally angry and in tumult inside all the time, and it takes just a spark to ignite them. Anger is often hiding some inner hurt.

Negative reaction

You become angry too. You start an exchange of abuse and aggression that feeds on itself. Angry words are an exchange of energy, so when someone attacks you they are actually stealing your energy. When you retaliate you are stealing it back. This tit-for-tat goes on until either person backs down. It is both disruptive and hurtful for both people involved and also for onlookers, especially children, for whom their parents are the prime role models for their future lives.

Positive reaction

Turn the other cheek. See the hurt inside the other person and find compassion for them. Tell any teenagers in your life to create their own values and standards and point out the dangers of being manipulated by peer pressure. Treat them as individuals having a valid point to make and listen to what they have to say, even if you don't agree with them.

With angry children check that they are not eating food to which they have a sensitivity, for example anything containing colour additives and preservatives can make children hyperactive and disturbed.

If you share your life with an angry adult be as tolerant as you can. Look at your own reaction: without consciously knowing it you may be the cause of some of the other person's anger – by condemning them you may be antagonising and making the situation worse. All you can do is try to change your attitude towards them and their behaviour. Sometimes this is enough to make them change. But if their anger is overwhelming your own life then take steps to move on.

It is virtually impossible to change someone else – an adult will rarely change unless they take on the responsibility of the change themselves. But you can change and you can decide how much you will take.

If you feel strongly on a subject voice your opinions but do it in a calm and moderate way – without aggression. If you feel so passionate that you can't speak calmly, wait until you have cooled a little then have your say. If you are being dominated or bullied by someone, get your thoughts together and think about your position. Then stand up for yourself in a controlled manner – your arguments and viewpoints will be far more effective than if you scream and shout your feelings in an unstructured way.

Stubbornness

People who are stubborn rarely admit they are wrong. They are frightened to say 'I've changed my mind' or to be seen to change direction from a previously expressed view. They fear that people will mock them or think less of them if they are seen to back down. They don't want to lose face. Their stubbornness could well be hiding a lack of self-esteem, for if we are confident about ourselves and our self-worth then we have no problem saying 'I'm wrong'.

Negative reaction

You spend too much time trying to change the person's mind. You become exasperated and then angry with them. The more you try to impose force upon them the more determinedly they will stick to their guns.

Positive reaction

My dog Prince was quite stubborn at times. If I tried to get him to go somewhere where he didn't want to go he would be just like the proverbial mule. The way for me to get him to move was to cajole him and make him feel safe. Once he lost the feeling of being threatened then he would move. People are like this – they are often frightened of change, preferring not to move rather than facing something unknown.

Some people have a lot of pride that makes them fearful of losing face so they will stick to their view even if presented with a better option simply because they don't want to look weak. Sometimes it is better to let the person feel at first that they have won, then at some later time gently persuade them to follow the alternative route.

I also find that timing is important when tackling someone who is stubborn or has fixed views – catch them in a good mood and manage the approach so that they think that it is actually their idea to follow some untried option. It is a deception, but a minor one and justified for its positive ends – helping the person to become open to new possibilities.

Over-emotionality and tearfulness

It's good to show your emotions but when someone is forever bursting into tears or swinging from laughter to tears and back it is quite difficult to know how to handle them. I have heard many men say that emotions are hard for them to cope with in an office or business situation. An emotional woman frightens most men. Of course, women don't have the monopoly on emotional behaviour. People can be emotional because of hormone imbalance or because they are having problems and pain in their life. Either way it's not much fun for them.

Negative reaction

Telling the person to pull themselves together and stop crying. If the person is truly upset this will only make them worse. Any anger or frustration you show towards them will aggravate the situation.

If you are working with an emotional person I suggest you do not get too involved in their personal affairs. People who are regularly emotional or overwrought are often looking for a stronger character to help them along. If you get too close to the situation you may become that person's crutch and then they will start to depend upon you. This will ultimately weaken them further and also be very draining for you too.

Don't, however, jump to conclusions about why the person is upset – their emotional episodes may be triggered by minor incidents and seem like oversensitivity but they may well be keeping something bottled up that is really a serious problem. You will feel very guilty if you are short with them or dismissive of their state without knowing the full situation.

Positive reaction

Offer sympathy, a shoulder to cry on (and tissues) for the first couple of times. Don't ask too many questions about the problem but if the emotional outbursts persist suggest they talk to a good counsellor or to the welfare officer at work if you have one. If the person works with you find out if there are any work-related problems that are causing the outbursts. Maybe their job is too demanding or is conflicting with their home life. Show compassion and understanding at all times. You may also suggest they take Bach Flower Remedies (see Chapter 2) and keep a bottle of Bach Rescue Remedy to hand as this is particularly good at calming down the emotions after a shock or upset.

Self-pity

This is the most draining of personality types to cope with. People who feel sorry for themselves are energy thieves. They will talk to you for hours about their problems then leave you drained of energy. Of course, we all have bouts of self-pity in our lives but I am talking here of people who are perpetually looking for someone to listen to their woes. You will be able to identify them:

- They tell you the same story over and over again, even when you have shown sympathy and caring on each occasion.
- They rarely follow any of the advice you give them.
- You hear them telling the same tales to every other person who is willing to listen.
- They consider themselves to be victims of circumstance and show no indications that they are prepared to take responsibility for what happens in their life.

Negative reaction

Sympathising may seem like a kind way to react but unfortunately it is one of the least helpful – it will feed the person's inability to take control of their life. Taking them into your life and family may also seem like a positive action but it has the opposite effect – the person will be even more confirmed in their dependency and your entire family will all be completely drained rather than just you.

Positive reaction

Put yourself into your egg (see exercise at the end of this chapter) and protect yourself from the energy drain. Without being unkind, be firm with the person. Buy him or her a book on self-help and propose ways that they can create their own life and heal themselves. Suggest professional help.

Sulking

Persistent sulkers are also energy thieves. Sulkers are usually looking for attention and are also very manipulative. However, just check that someone you perceive as a sulker isn't suffering from a genuine injustice. If the person is part of a family in which he or she has been verbally or physically abused, he or she will often become withdrawn and unsociable – this is not sulking but psychological self-protection, shutting down emotions to avoid emotional harm.

Sulking is where a person who doesn't get their own way makes obvious signs to all around that he or she is upset. Sulkers only perform to audiences. Sulking is petulance. It is the behaviour of self-absorbed people, because they don't care too much about the effect their behaviour has on other people. It is a behaviour pattern more likely found in the home than in the office.

Negative reaction

Retaliation – slamming doors and showing signs of petulance yourself. This will just exhaust you and if my experience of this type of behaviour is anything to go by it will develop into a battle of silence – a trial of who can last the longest without talking.

Positive reaction

As soon as you are sure that there is nothing truly wrong then ignore the performance. Get into your egg. The more attention the sulker gets, the more they will continue the game.

Egotistical behaviour

This is the behaviour of a person who wants the world to orientate itself around them. A person who believes they are important – not to be confused with one who knows themselves and accepts themselves for what they are, whether good or bad. Egotists tend to bore people with their own importance. They can be snobs. They are often selfish – considering only themselves. Egotists will not care for the feelings of others – they will be concerned with their own comforts and will want to win all arguments and have their way in all decision-making situations. You will know when you have met one – you will feel emotionally steamrollered.

Actually I have met very few genuine egotists. Most people I know have problems accepting that they are worthy, and issues with self-respect and self-worth are more prevalent than egotism. I think today's schooling and social system are unlikely to allow anyone to build up their ego and self-importance too much. Peer pressure tends to bring down any sign of elitism fairly quickly.

We are not encouraged to lord it over others or shout our own praises.

Negative reaction

You argue with them. This will lead to acrimony and an even worse atmosphere. An egotist will never concede that they are wrong so arguing is a waste of time.

Positive reaction

Use any opportunity to show them what they are like. Personally I would avoid them.

Low self-esteem

People who have low self-esteem or little self-respect can be very draining. They will be constantly seeking approval and will have very little confidence. They may show signs of self-pity. They will often have secondary problems as a result of their own lack of self-love – they may have problems making decisions, develop eating disorders or other sicknesses, lean on those near to them for moral and emotional support, find it difficult to engage socially and be disinclined to join in group activities.

They can also be so keen to gain approval that they may drive themselves too hard to reach an unattainable perfection. These traits will all be quite trying for those around them, whether family members or work colleagues.

Negative reaction

Attempting to make their decisions for them or letting them become dependent on you will just make them weaker and less empowered, undermining their self-esteem even further.

Positive reaction

Find ways to help them to act independently and empower themselves. Encourage them in their creativity as achievement of any kind will raise their self-esteem and self-confidence. Show them respect and honour them and try not to mock or belittle them at any time. Encourage them to take on self-responsibility. Tell them that they are important and that they have their own unique qualities.

Fearfulness

Fear is a very negative emotion. It creates negativity like nothing else apart from hatred. An anxious and fearful person is difficult to live or work with because they will drain you of energy and will be reluctant to move forward in life. Their lives are limited by their fears and anxieties. They will often have low self-esteem and there is the chance that they will develop panic attacks, paranoia and other serious psychological and mental problems. Some fears arise from clear and obvious sources, others are unreasonable. Some fear can be attributed to trauma, where a person has died and the emotional scars remain.

Negative reaction

To dismiss the fears and tell the person to pull themselves together. Very often people who are extremely fearful are unable to control their fears so telling them to 'get over it' will not help. Nor should you ignore or laugh at the person. Panic attacks are ghastly experiences not to be dismissed as fanciful and certainly not to be mocked.

Positive reaction
You will need tolerance and understanding when dealing with this problem. Offer help to the person either by listening to their fears and worries yourself or, if you feel that they need professional help, by gently suggesting that they visit a counsellor, a conventional medical doctor, or a complementary healer. Complementary therapies that can help to clear fears include energy healing, acupuncture and past life regression.

Smothering love

This is the habit of stifling a person with possessive love and is a typical partner or parental problem – you probably won't encounter it in the workplace. Mostly it is associated with mothers. The sort of thing it involves are, say, continually asking how you are, or forever checking on your movements and saying things like 'I was worrying about you, dear'.

Smotherers seem to be full of care for you but in reality their love is overwhelming and suffocating – like a soft yet heavy and unyielding blanket. Their love is often conditional and manipulative ('Oh, don't worry if you can't come, I suppose I'll have to manage somehow', 'You wouldn't do this if you really cared about me') and can create feelings of guilt in the receiver. You feel guilty because you are not returning their love in the same all-consuming way. You feel guilty because you want to run away from it to avoid being taken over – and indeed a person with, say, a smothering parent will often end up making their own home as far away as possible.

The person who tries to control and own a person in this way is lacking self-esteem and self-confidence and has either been treated in this way themselves or, more likely, has experienced a lack of love. They are fearful of losing the person they are smothering – although their behaviour is very likely to make this happen.

Negative reaction

Show your irritation and reject them. Get angry. Move away.

Positive reaction

This needs careful handling. The person who smothers is often someone near and dear to you. Look into their past and see if you can discover why they are behaving this way. If they haven't received love themselves then try to get across to them that you love them and that they have nothing to fear. Try to explain as kindly as you can that you would rather have some space and that you find their overwhelming care too much to take. Like the Arab holding the desert sand, if you keep your hand open the sand will stay but if you hold it tight it will fall out. When you visit the person, get into your egg.

Dithering

Ditherers are people who lack the confidence to make up their minds. They find it incredibly difficult to reach a decision because they are forever looking at all the alternatives. They are out of touch with their intuition and are letting fear stop them listening to their inner self. Therefore all options feel the same to them, and they can't trust their feelings to help them make decisions on what is right or wrong for them. Often they are worrying about the outcome and how it will be perceived in the eyes of others. Ditherers can be very infuriating and a true test of your patience.

Negative reaction
Show your irritation. Make up their minds for them.

Positive reaction
Ditherers are fearful and will benefit from some sensitive help and guidance. Make sure you get into your egg to prevent yourself being drained by them. Show patience and present the options to them as clearly and succinctly as possible. Help them to sense what they genuinely and instinctively feel about each option rather than what they think they *ought* to do. Encourage them to look at each option properly and look at the potential outcome. Tell them to be less controlling of the future, help them to 'let go' and 'go with the flow' – reassure them that whatever the outcome or result of their choice it will be OK.

Unreliability

Unreliable people are frustrating to work with and annoying socially. They often cannot arrive on time and forget appointments and meetings. If you always keep people waiting it can come across as a lack of care and even as selfish – 'my time is more important than your time'. Very often unreliable people are not able to say no to anyone and overfill their lives. If someone regularly makes promises and forgets to fulfil them or otherwise doesn't perform they are also showing themselves to be careless of your trust.

Negative reaction
Keep saying 'It's OK, it doesn't matter' – when it does matter to you very much.

Positive reaction

Tell the person that you don't think it's acceptable to keep on letting you down. Insist that you are not going to be treated in that way. Tell them what it feels like to be kept waiting over and over again – sometimes people genuinely don't see how it affects others. Buy them a book on time management.

Over-zealousness

This is not always necessarily a negative state – over-zealous people are often the 'movers and shakers' of the world and may leave a positive mark – they are often those that turn situations around and work with good causes. Still, their energy can be very draining for those who come into contact with them. They are often living in the fast lane and crash through our lives creating tidal waves of backlash energy. Such people often have sacred cows – objects of devotion – and can put people and issues on pedestals. They can be 'wired', hyperactive, chaotic and undisciplined and quite difficult to live with. They may also occasionally be egotistical.

Negative reaction

Try to compete. Try to stand in their way and stop them. Try to put them down. It's very tempting to try and destabilise someone who seems so sure of themselves and where they are going.

Positive reaction

Take cover! Allow the person to be themselves and move out of their way. See their good points – their zeal may be furthering a good cause – and be tolerant. Don't let them suck you into their issues and situations unless you want to be their lackey – if you can't match their extreme levels of enthusiasm you will always be running in their wake. Put yourself in your egg and concentrate on your own life.

Protecting Yourself from Negative Energy

Having now identified some of the main negative personal characteristics and behaviour patterns you may encounter in your life, what can you do to protect yourself from them?

Protective visualisations

In the same way that thoughts affect your energy, the intention to protect yourself will strengthen your energy field. There are a number of simple visualisation techniques you can use to preserve and protect yourself when you are in the presence of disruptive and draining energies.

The egg

This is a very simple but effective way to protect your aura and personal space from other people's emotional outbursts or negative thoughts. It takes only a few seconds to visualise. I suggest that you get into your egg whenever you encounter any of the energy types mentioned above, and also when you visit hospitals and other places where people are sick or needy.

EXERCISE: STEPPING INTO THE EGG

- Imagine yourself stepping into a large egg. Step in through a doorway and close the door behind you.

- The egg has thick walls that keep out all negative emotions.
- Know that these walls will protect you, and only love will come through.
- Put as many windows as you wish into the walls of your egg.
- If you are in an ongoing contentious situation then renew your egg every few hours. Otherwise visualising it every morning will be fine.

An alternative to the egg is the bubble – a big, clear bubble around you that again keeps out negativity. You can see through it and positive energies can penetrate to you, but anything negative just hits the outside and bounces back.

The garage door

This is a protection specifically against outbursts of anger. When you unexpectedly see someone angry coming towards you, or clearly about to direct anger at you, then imagine an up-and-over garage door slamming down in front of you. You are effectively putting up a barrier to the emotional stream of negativity and stopping it from reaching your energy field. Appropriately, this is a good method to use when you are on the receiving end of road rage. By not reacting to the other person's anger you will be helping to diffuse it.

The golden pyramid

You can use this protection technique on yourself or other people. It is good when you feel you are about to enter a difficult situation where you may encounter aggression, hatred, anger or jealousy. It can also protect you against curses and other forms of psychic attack (see Chapter 7).

Visualise yourself inside a golden pyramid. Try to see a three-dimensional pyramid if you can, but if not then just imagine yourself standing within a golden triangle. This is also a great way to keep your loved ones safe – visualise them inside the pyramid as they go off on their journeys or when you especially want to keep them away from harm.

The silver cloak

Imagine yourself putting on a reflective silver cloak. This will make you invincible and protect you from negative energy streams.

Crystals and amulets

Crystals are useful for protecting us from all levels and types of negative energy. They can also help us neutralise the effects of mobile phones and electrical pollution (we will be looking at all these potentially harmful situations in later chapters). Crystals have their own energy fields and vibrations and these can counteract any negative fields and emissions. Each crystal type has a unique vibration that affects the atmosphere in an different way. Here are some crystals that can deflect negativity from you through their subtle but powerful energy emissions:

- Aegirine
- Black tourmaline
- Jasper
- Jet
- Malachite
- Smoky quartz

Before you start to use a crystal you should cleanse it then recharge it. There are several ways to cleanse crystals:

- Wash the crystal in a mix of mineral water and rock salt and leave it standing in the solution for several hours or overnight. Throw away the salt water after use.
- Wash the crystal in the sea or fresh running water like a stream or waterfall.
- Place the crystal in the earth for at least 24 hours.
- Leave the crystal out in the rain – a thunderstorm is even better, as it will recharge the crystal as well.
- Hold the crystal in the smoke of a burning incense stick. Sandalwood and sage are particularly good for releasing negativity.
- If a crystal has been heavily used for clearing and protecting put it in a bowl of sea salt and leave for several days. Throw away the salt after use.

Once the crystal is cleansed rinse it under running water. You then need to recharge it in one of the following ways:

- Leave the crystal in the Sun for a few hours.
- Put it out in a thunderstorm (unless you have already cleansed it in this way – see above).
- Leave it overnight under the light of the Moon – especially a full Moon.
- Place it on a large crystal cluster for a few hours.
- Charge it with the healing symbol (see Chapter 2).

You should regularly cleanse and recharge any crystals that you wear or have in your home or office, at least once a month. If you don't they will become full and will lose their efficacy for clearing the atmosphere.

EXERCISE: PROTECT YOURSELF WITH CLEAR QUARTZ

You can 'programme' a clear quartz crystal to protect you and dissipate all negative energies around you.

- Cleanse the crystal and charge it.
- Hold it in your hand and make a positive statement along the lines of 'all negative and misaligned energies are repelled'. Say the statement three times.
- Carry the crystal with you in your bag or pocket for protection, or alternatively put it by your bed.
- Every three months cleanse, recharge and reprogramme your crystal.

Cleansing Yourself of Negative Energy

If you have been unable to avoid contamination by negative energies there are ways that you can clear them. You will know if you have been affected if you find that you are tired and sluggish, or generally out of sorts.

I get a 'muzzy' head and suddenly feel very disinclined to do very much at all. My limbs are heavy and I feel as though I have a hangover. You may also get a full-blown headache or feel very nervous for no real reason. Your mind may start racing and you may be unable to sleep. It's quite common to have a general feeling of heaviness, especially around your shoulders, as though you have picked up a great weight.

There are a number of ways in which you can personally clear yourself and your surroundings. Try them and find the methods that suit you and your circumstances best. Make it a habit to cleanse yourself regularly to prevent the effects of negative energy from accumulating.

Salt baths

If you have been badly affected by negative energy a salt bath is wonderful for clearing and cleansing yourself. Sea salt is the best type of salt to use but Epsom salts also work well. Salt attracts negative energy and will draw it away from you. A salt bath is especially good if you have been in a violent or disturbing situation, and if you are a healer or carer it is great for clearing away the effects of the people you have been helping. It is also good to use after a long journey.

Smudging

Whenever I visited a friend of mine in his Hong Kong apartment he would make me stand at the entrance while he 'smudged' me with smouldering sage. He is a Native American and follows the traditions of his ancestors with this ancient cleansing practice, which his people use in their rituals and ceremonies. The smoke is the cleansing agent and although it is quite pungent and not to everyone's taste, using it is the most effective and quick-acting way to clear negativity that I know.

You can buy sage from many mind, body and spirit shops in its natural state – not dried and powdered for cooking. It comes in the form of sage twigs bound together in a bundle. You light the bundle and allow it to smoulder. As it smoulders you wave the smoke all around yourself or you can get a friend to do it for you.

Make sure you hold a bowl underneath to catch any smouldering bits of twig (Native Americans traditionally use an abalone shell to hold the twigs). You can also use smudging as a method for cleansing particular possessions which might hold negative energy, whether it be your clothes, your car or your entire home. Wave the smoke from the smouldering sage throughout the entire house, paying particular attention to the corners, where negative energy can build up (see also Chapter 5).

Aromatherapy oils for cleansing and clearing

Certain aromatherapy oils have excellent energy-cleansing properties. You can use them in burners (suspended in a little water so they are widely dispersed by the steam), in the bath (they disperse better if mixed with a tiny amount of milk), or mixed with water to make a fine spray for use in rooms or on particular possessions. There are many oils but I especially recommend the following, which are widely available.

- **Cedarwood** Known for clearing anxiety and stress. Use in a burner.
- **Eucalyptus** Particularly good for clearing your head. Put a few drops on your pillow or on a tissue by your head at night, or add a few drops to a steam inhalation – this will also clear a congested nose.
- **Juniper** A great cleanser of negative energies. Put some on your wrists and hands then brush your hands through your aura, sweeping down towards your feet. Breathe the aroma deeply.
- **Lime** Also very effective for clearing negativity. I use a lime shower gel and I find it makes me feel really clear and revitalised.
- **Orange** Very refreshing. Use it in the bath or burn it to clear your home.
- **Sage** Like sage in its natural state, the oil extracted from the shrub is a very powerful cleanser and very stimulating. Use in a burner or, as with eucalyptus, add a few drops to a steam inhalation.

- **Sandalwood** Well known for its clearing and cleansing properties, sandalwood also has a lovely smell. Use in a burner in your home or place of work.

Running water

If you live in a hot climate, standing under a natural waterfall is the most wonderful way to clean away the toxins of negative thought forms and it will revitalise you like nothing else. However, for those of us who live in a cooler climate a shower will have to suffice.

First rub a little sea salt over your skin, then apply one of the above essential oils mixed in a carrier such as almond oil. Next, scrub your body under the shower and visualise your entire being washed clean. If you focus your intention on letting go you will find your morning shower can be a spiritual, mental and emotional cleansing as well as a physical one.

Crystals for chakra balancing

All crystals and gemstones work on releasing our emotional blocks and issues. When we use the crystals we have already looked at for energy protection they will also be helping us to clear our personal energy field. However, there is a particular way in which we can use crystals that will bring our entire being back into balance.

The body has seven main energy points called 'chakras' (the word *chakra* is Sanskrit for 'wheel'). As their name suggests these are points of spinning energy, and when they are in their ideal healthy state they spin in a perfect circle. However, the chakras can become distorted and misaligned when we have been affected by any form of negative energy, whether from within ourselves or from an external source. It is very rare for anyone to have perfectly balanced chakras apart from enlightened beings like Jesus and the Buddha, but we can work on improving them and keeping them in balance.

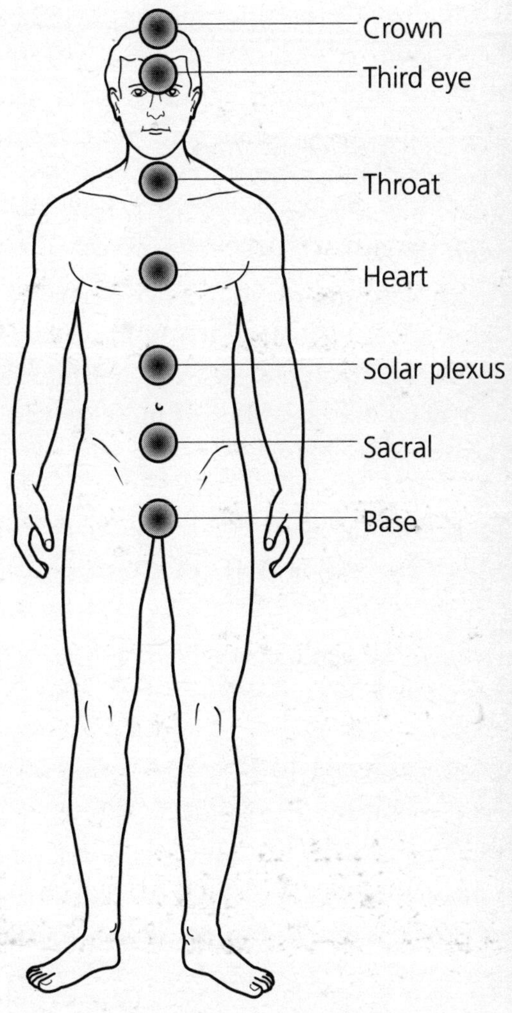

There are seven chakras (energy centres) in the body, from the crown chakra at the top of the head to the base chakra at the bottom of the spine.

Crystals are wonderful for helping us to clear our chakras because the vibrations of crystal energy counteract and neutralise any negativity and help bring our energy centres back into balance. Many crystals can work on the different chakras but I have chosen a set here that you should have no difficulty in finding in your nearest crystal shop. All you need are small stones – about a centimetre in diameter will be fine. Here is a list of the chakras and the crystals that you can use to clear and balance each one:

Crown chakra

Location The top of your head.
Crystal Clear quartz. This stone brings harmony and strength. It is a potent healing crystal as it connects you to universal energies. It will increase the power and size of your energy field.

'Third eye' chakra

Location On your forehead between and just above your eyebrows.
Crystal Amethyst, a peaceful stone that quietens the mind and helps you to meditate.

Throat chakra

Location Below your windpipe in the dip of your clavicle.
Crystal Blue lace agate. This is a calming and cooling stone that is good for open communication and for bones.

Heart chakra

Location In the centre of your chest.
Crystal Rose quartz, which will open you to receive and

give love. It will help heal the heart after the loss of a loved one. It also allows you to release suppressed emotions.

Solar plexus chakra
Location Just below your ribs.
Crystal Citrine, for happiness and prosperity. It also brings peace and calm and disperses negative energy.

Sacral chakra
Location Just below your belly button.
Crystal Carnelian, which is a good healer for the lower body. It will ward off other people's anger and help to shift in-bred patterns and attitudes as well as negativity from difficult experiences.

Base chakra
Location At the base of your spine.
Crystal Black tourmaline, which will strengthen your immune system and is a powerful repellent of negative energies.

EXERCISE: CHAKRA BALANCING WITH CRYSTALS

- Cleanse and charge the crystals before you use them (see the section a little earlier in the chapter).
- Find a quiet spot and put on some relaxing music.
- Lying down, position the appropriate crystal on each chakra. For the crystals to be most effective place them directly on the skin at the correct point or wear cotton or another natural fibre and place them on top of your clothing. Obviously if you are lying down you can't put the crown chakra crystal on the top of your head, but you can place it on the ground against your

head. Place the base chakra crystal underneath you at the bottom of your spine.

- Once the crystals are in position totally relax and let them do their work.

Remember to cleanse the crystals after use.

Apache tears

I was introduced to apache tears by the same Native American friend who showed me how to smudge with sage. A type of obsidian, apache tears are small, round, almost black pebbles of volcanic glass found in the beds of streams and rivers where they have become smooth from the constant washing of the water.

The Native Americans used them to clear away any negative thoughts, grief or troubles that they wished to release. They would take an apache tear out into the desert and throw it over their shoulder, letting go of their problem at the same time. You can do the same, but if there isn't a desert near you I find it most exhilarating to throw the stones into the sea or a river. This means there is also less chance of someone else picking up your troubles.

EXERCISE: LETTING GO OF PROBLEMS

- Hold an apache tear in your hand.
- Imagine your problem or troubles going into the crystal.
- Throw the crystal over your shoulder and know that you are letting go of your burden for good.

If you are interested in learning more about crystals there are many good books on the market, but good starter books are Judy Hall's *Illustrated Guide to Crystals* and Soozi Holbeche's *The Power of Crystals* (see Further Reading, page 282).

Symbol for releasing negative energy

The release symbol below will release blocks and thought forms and can be used on yourself or other people. The release symbol can be combined with the aura-combing process described in Chapter 2 to help you to clear, relax, unwind, destress and balance yourself.

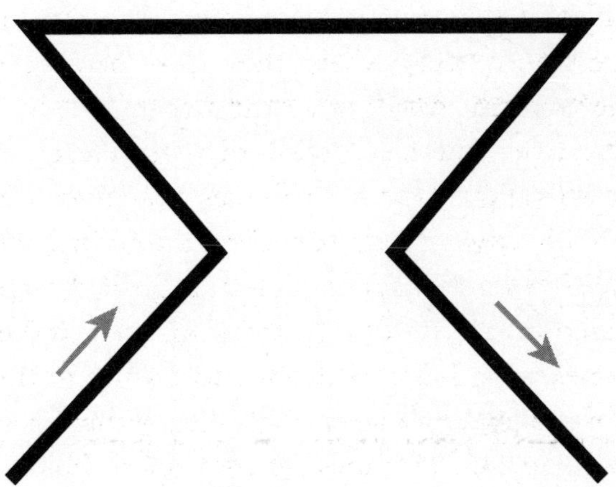

To clear energy blocks, draw the release symbol in the air three times over the affected area. So if you have a stuffed-up nose draw it over your nose; if your head is muzzy or aching then draw it in front of your face.

EXERCISE: RELEASING NEGATIVE ENERGY WITH THE RELEASE SYMBOL

- 'Comb' through your aura from top to bottom for a few minutes, using your hands as a comb and flicking

the negative energy into a bowl of salt water.
- Draw the healing symbol three times in the air in front of you.
- Place your hands on each of your chakras in turn, starting with the base chakra and moving up to the crown chakra. Let your hands rest on each chakra for a few minutes. You can also combine this exercise with the chakra-balancing exercise using crystals – placing your hands over the crystals will magnify their effects.

Developing Personal Boundaries

Although we are all connected by the energies of life, we are all unique and to remain so we need to hold on to our individuality. To do this we have to avoid being affected by the people around us, by ensuring that our own individuality is clearly delineated and marked out. In much the same way that animals stake out their territory, we need to make sure that our personal aura and space are protected.

We have looked at various ways of protecting our personal energy field. However, the most effective method of protection is to be completely clear – both to ourselves and to those around us – about our own individual status, our personal essence, our unique identity.

Open up to your inner self

The key to establishing a strong identity is to make contact with your intuition, which will tell you what is truly right for you. Connect to your intuition by opening up to your feelings and senses. Practise sensing the difference between truth and falsehood (or self-deception) by observing how your body reacts whenever you make a decision – eventually you will know immediately when you have made the right choice for yourself. A choice that is truly right will make you feel strong, while one that is not completely right will make you feel weak, or give you butterflies, or generate other signs of nerves.

Voicing your feelings and thoughts clearly and emphatically – without being narrow-minded, overbearing or dogmatic – and following your intuition at all times will help you to establish your own identity. This will create strong etheric boundaries for all your bodies – physical, mental, spiritual and emotional – and this will create a highly effective barrier between your energy field and the energies of others and the environment.

Respect yourself

Part of the process of creating strong personal boundaries is making sure you look after yourself and respect yourself at all times. This means that occasionally you will need to say no to the demands of others. This can be tricky in a home environment, especially when there are people involved whom we love and who have needs. However, if you give your all to other people you will weaken yourself. Love, care and help others as much as you can – but always keep some time and energy for yourself.

Exercise: Healing Visualisation to Clear Your Aura

To end this section on counteracting and clearing the effects of other people's negativity I offer you this three-part visualisation exercise, for which you will need pen, paper and coloured pencils or crayons.

Stage 1

In the first part of the exercise you use your intuition in order to imagine your aura and to sense any negativity that you may have picked up either from others or from your own thought patterns and habits.

- Take a pen and paper and draw a simple outline of yourself.
- Draw another outline around the first indicating what you imagine to be the shape and extent of your aura.
- Do you feel that there are any blocks and thought forms anywhere in your aura? If so, outline how you imagine their shape and size to be at the relevant points in your aura.
- Now colour in your aura as you imagine it to look. If you have difficulty imagining this use the first colour that comes into your head – don't think about it but make your choice an automatic, instinctive reaction. Colour in any blocks and thought forms as well.

Stage 2

The following visualisation will use your mind and intention to clear any blocks and negativity from your aura.

- Find a quiet place where you will not be disturbed. Sit comfortably on a chair. Relax.
- Close your eyes and breathe into the very depth of your lungs. Inhale and exhale slowly.
- Feel your feet becoming heavier and heavier. Feel as though they are magnetised and completely connected to the ground beneath you.
- Let your entire body relax and become soft.

- Visualise a beautiful violet flame burning all around you.
- Pause for a while, letting the flame burn away all the negativity from your own thoughts and from the thoughts of others. See it burn up everything that has bothered you over the last few days.
- Direct the flame to the blocks and thought forms you have identified in your aura.
- Take a few minutes to ensure your aura is now clear.
- See a beam of white light descending from the sky to fill your aura and your body. Breathe in this light. Soak yourself in it. Become totally immersed in it.
- Now look down and visualise a beautiful silver cloak lying on the ground. Pick it up and know that this will protect you from the negativity of others.
- Now that you have such a powerful protection, feel yourself growing strong and confident. You can withstand anything now – nobody can affect you with their thoughts or emotions. You are completely protected from negativity.
- Breathe deeply for a few moments before slowly opening your eyes.

Stage 3

- Take another sheet of paper and draw how you now imagine your aura to be. It should now be free from blocks and negative spots. If there are any left then repeat the exercise over the following days until your aura becomes clearer.
- Now draw two bold outlines around your aura showing the boundaries of your space.
- Tell yourself that these boundaries are there not only to protect you from negativity but also to ensure that you keep some space and energy for yourself at all times.

So far we have looked at how our own negative thoughts, attitudes and behaviour and those of others can affect our well-being. However, it is not only people who can have a negative influence – there are also many sources of negative energy in the environment around us. In the following chapters we will look at these and how we can best control or avoid them. To start with let's look at the direct physical source of most of our energy – our food and drink.

4

Negative Energies in Food and Drink

We are now going to see how what we eat and drink can affect our well-being. I will be looking at different types of food and how they are produced and prepared, and showing you ways in which you can effectively avoid, or at least live with, the most harmful aspects of negativity in food. We will conclude with a physical detox that will cleanse you of any toxicity that may have accumulated in your system – allowing you to clear the past and start anew.

How Food Affects Us

As the saying goes 'we are what we eat', and there is no doubt that we are affected by the food we consume. It is, of course, our food and drink that provides us with the energy to fuel our physical body and the power to get through our daily activities.

Everyone will agree that it is essential that we have a constant supply of good-quality food and drink, but our definition of the word 'good' may vary. What is your perception of good food? Have you been won over by the greens and believe that you should eat organic food? Are you a vegetarian or maybe even a vegan or macrobiotic eater? Is your idea of a good meal the traditional 'meat and two veg' – no matter where it comes from? Or are you a fast-food junkie?

I admit that I personally love the occasional veggie burger and milkshake. However, I keep myself under control most of the time as although tasty such foods are so processed that they are not the most nutritious food and they are high in calories.

Without getting too technical, calories are simply the units we use to measure the energy that our body will receive from a particular item of food. For you to be healthy and have a reasonable chance of getting through the day without exhaustion you need 2,000 calories per day if you are a grown woman and 2,500 calories if you are a man. This assumes you pursue normal activities – obviously someone who ran five miles a day would need more.

The Food We Eat

Basically, I consider 'good' food to be food that provides us with uncontaminated and clear energy. That is why I believe it is important to consider your eating habits, so that you gain not just energy from what you eat but *positive* energy.

In the days when we grew much of our own food and cooked our own meals, used natural fertilisers and took our chances with the small pests that attacked our food, the energy we derived from food was clear and pure. Provided we had enough of it, it supplied us with all we needed to be healthy.

Animals were kept in natural conditions and were usually humanely, swiftly and skilfully slaughtered on the farm where they lived rather than being transported many miles to factory-style abattoirs. The local butcher almost invariably got his supplies from the local farmer, and the stress involved for the animals was minimal. As we will see, for the most part it's a different story these days. We will now look at how our food is produced, beginning with food derived from animals.

Meat and poultry

First of all I should tell you where I am coming from. I am a vegetarian, so I don't eat meat, including chicken and fish. I have to spell this out, because many restaurants think that vegetarians will still eat chicken, or at least fish. So let's make this clear – a vegetarian only eats vegetables, together with the *products* of animals such as milk, cheese and eggs. A vegan, on the other hand, avoids anything that is derived from animals in any way, including eggs and dairy produce as well as leather and bone china cups.

I became a vegetarian some six years ago when I suddenly couldn't face the idea of putting any form of flesh into my mouth. The whole idea of eating something that had lived became abhorrent to me. However, if you do eat meat I strongly advise you to check on the conditions in which the animals are kept and slaughtered.

Farming practices

I do not believe it can be good for us to eat the flesh of beings that have been kept in unnatural conditions and fed unnaturally. I belong to several organisations that support humane farming practices and I am appalled at the photographs they have taken showing the misery and cruelty that so many animals suffer when bred and reared in factory farm conditions. Some of them are herded into small enclosures where they remain for many months of the year and in some cases through their entire lives.

I understand that farmers must bring herds of cattle in for the winter for their own sakes and this is not the issue here. It's the factory farm concept of keeping animals and birds in enclosed conditions throughout their entire lives that upsets me. Such practices are still used in Europe and in many parts of the world. For example, veal is produced by keeping a calf without light throughout its short life so that its meat stays white.

Until recently most chickens in Britain were reared in overcramped batteries, large indoor cages where they are fattened in their thousands until taken for slaughter. A law has now been passed, thanks to the efforts of the supporters of animal welfare, banning the use of the worst types of battery cage in Britain.

By nature cows and sheep are herbivores, feeding mainly on grass. But their diet may be supplemented with manufactured feed that contains parts of other cows and sheep left over from the slaughtering process. This enforced cannibalism causes discord and disharmony within the animals' energy fields – and these negative emotions will, of course, then be passed to whoever eats their meat. And that is not all that may be passed on.

The use of infected cow parts in cattle feed was the

cause of the epidemic of bovine spongiform encephalopathy (BSE) – 'mad cow disease' – in Britain in the late 1980s and 1990s, which was transmitted to humans in the form of variant Creuzfeldt-Jakob disease (vCJD). We don't yet know the full effects of vCJD, which can incubate in the body for over a decade. In Britain, the use of animal products in animal feed is now banned.

The slaughtering of animals is also a problem. In Britain the government has closed down a lot of the smaller abattoirs around the country and animals have to be transported over long distances. This causes great distress to the transported animals and also makes it difficult to contain outbreaks of infectious diseases – it was the main cause of the devastating epidemic of foot-and-mouth disease that hit Britain in 2001, leading to the mass slaughter of hundreds of thousands of animals considered to be at risk.

The holding, transportation and marketing conditions of live animals everywhere in the world seems to have little respect for the animals' well-being. I have seen sheep and cows absolutely terrified in markets where they are jostled and pushed and very often encouraged to move by the use of an electric prod. Can you imagine their fear as they enter an abattoir and sense the fear of the animals that have already been killed before them?

Fear has a similar effect on animals as it does on us. Their entire bodies are affected – just think how you would feel when faced with a life-threatening situation – every part of you tenses up and becomes rigid and every cell of your body will be affected by the fear. So it is for animals, and the longer they are in this state of fear, the more pronounced the effects will be.

How can the meat of an animal that experiences such fear as it dies be good for you? For a start, on a physical level, the meat will be full of stress hormones released by the creature's body as it experiences fear. The negativity stays in the meat. It is well to remember that those neat, sanitised little packages that you buy from the supermarket are the essence of a living being that may have faced slaughter in a state of abject, uncomprehending terror.

Organic farming

Fortunately there are now many farmers who also see that such practices are not the way ahead and many are now adopting organic methods. 'Organic' in the context of cattle and poultry rearing means that the animals are allowed to roam free whenever possible and are fed on food that does not contain chemical pesticides or the meat of other animals. Animals reared organically have had a good and natural life and are fed with suitable food. Unlike non-organic herds or flocks they are not routinely injected with antibiotics and growth hormones, which remain in the meat.

If you eat meat then I would advise you to choose organic, even if it is a little more expensive. If eating out, ask if the meat is organic, because only customer pressure will make restaurants change their own buying habits. By taking the organic option you at least have some reassurance that the animal has been reared in reasonable conditions and fed decent and appropriate food.

Fish

Fish is a great source of nutrition – an important source of protein – and is easier to digest than meat, especially red meat. However, most of us have had a bout of food poisoning from fish or seafood and know it is no fun. Unfortunately, our seas are contaminated now and we should take care about the source of these foods.

I lived in Hong Kong for a couple of years and while I was there the seas around the island became infested with what was called the 'Red Tide'. This was an infestation of algae that poisoned all the fish and shellfish in the area for months. It was a local tragedy, as many of the fishermen and shellfish farmers were put out of business. I don't know where it came from but the main theory was that it had been washed down rivers from the industrial belt of southern China.

This is not an unusual situation – many factories still spew their toxic waste into rivers and the sea. Also, many of the unprecedented number of industrial ships and boats at sea these days dump waste into the oceans. Shellfish are particularly vulnerable as they live in the mouths of estuaries and flourish in the gravel brought down by the rivers where toxic waste gathers. Many people I know are actually completely intolerant of shellfish and will always have side effects when they eat it.

If you suffer at all from bloating, nausea, rashes or any other symptoms when you eat seafood then I would advise you just to leave it out of your diet. Shellfish, especially oysters, that are farmed in enclosed and controlled conditions are safer, but these conditions are not natural and, like farmed salmon and trout, they are often pumped full of antibiotics. When you buy fresh or frozen fish I recommend examining the whole fish so that you can see its condition. If you see any sign of malformation, especially of the scales, don't buy it.

Dairy products

These days an increased number of people have an intolerance to dairy products. I am not a scientist but it would seem that this is very probably due to the pesticides used on the food that the cows eat and the drugs they are given to increase their yields. The best thing to do, again, is to look for the 'organic' label on milk and cheese.

Dairy intolerance will manifest itself in a noticeable increase in mucus in your nose, throat and chest after you have eaten food that includes milk, cream, cheese or yoghurt. A full allergy will have more serious effects such as vomiting and diarrhoea. I have a sensitivity to dairy products, which means that I try to cut down on my consumption. I find that I feel much better when I eat goat's cheese and drink goat's milk (which contain smaller fat globules than cow's milk and so are easier to digest) and rice milk or soya milk.

Vegetables

I saw a television programme a while ago that deeply disturbed me and made me realise how vulnerable we are to the farming practices over which we have no control. It was not a horror film in the conventional sense but a documentary about tomatoes, which told how several people had become ill and died from poison that was traced to tomatoes from a market garden in southern Spain. The tomatoes had been sprayed with a solution that contained poison – the deadly spray was probably to kill pests, or it may have been a mistake by the farmer.

Ever since I saw the film I have always washed my vegetables and fruits thoroughly. Washing with a diluted solution of vinegar is also said to ensure a thorough cleanse. Vegetables can be affected not only by the pesticides sprayed upon them but also by the toxicity of the soil in which they are grown. Years of applying chemical fertilisers and pesticides will leave the soil lifeless and toxic.

Again you will be safer buying vegetables with organic labels as this guarantees that the vegetables were grown in clear, non-toxic soil and not sprayed by harmful substances. If you cannot afford to go organic for all your vegetables, I recommend at least buying organic carrots and lettuces because the non-organic kind may have been sprayed with pesticides up to six times – more frequently than most other types of vegetable.

Nutrition and Nurture

We might speak of 'food like mother cooked' to describe the wholesome food that was cooked with love and care with the best interests of the family at heart. Our mothers and grandmothers traditionally prepared food as part of the nurturing process of motherhood. In some families today it might be the father who does the cooking as much as the mother, but whoever does it there is always a positive exchange of energy when we cook for those we love.

The food we buy in plastic containers at the supermarket and pop into the microwave, the food we get from the local takeaway and the food we eat in most restaurants is either prepared with a total lack of interest or, worse still, by machines. Who prepares your food?

In recent years there has generally been a growth in affordable eating out. More of us eat in restaurants than ever before, and in Britain most pubs now include a restaurant area or at least serve food. There has also been an increase in the ready-made food market for the many people who find they don't have the time or inclination to cook three meals a day from scratch from raw ingredients. However, there is a price to pay for eating food prepared by strangers.

I noticed in Malaysia that each village has one or two families who spend all their time cooking food that they sell at small stalls-cum-cafés, where the rest of the village can eat. Everyone knows the people cooking the food – they are all members of the same community and there is a sense of sharing. This is the same on the kibbutzim in Israel and in most other traditional communities.

However, in more modern societies and in cities we rarely know who has prepared and handled the food we buy in the shops. The ingredients of each meal may each have passed through many hands. This is fine if the people handling our food are happy and in a good frame of mind, but if they are unhappy, angry, anxious or even sick their negative vibrations will be transferred into the food and will be passed on to us as we eat it.

How can we bring the essential ingredient of love back into our food? How can we make sure that our meals are uncontaminated with negative energies? How can we raise the vibration of the food that we eat? One way is to bless it and heal it.

Blessing food

In the past the head of the household would say grace and bless the food before a meal. This in itself did a lot to neutralise any adverse energies that may have been picked up by the ingredients. The thankfulness we feel and express is a powerful positive vibration. Gratitude is an immensely uplifting emotion and will have a very beneficial effect on food. Here is a simple grace that you can use or adapt to suit the occasion:

We thank all those who have contributed to this meal.
We thank all those who farmed the land, planted the seed and grew these plants for our benefit.
We thank the animals that have offered themselves for our nourishment.
We thank God, the planet and all creation for the nurturing this food brings.

When you prepare food, remember to keep yourself in a positive state of mind as your thoughts and emotions will pass on into your meal, affecting everyone who eats it. Take a few minutes to calm yourself before you start.

How to heal food

Healing food raises its vibrations. It will not only clear away any negativity but also positively uplift its energies. You can use any form of energy healing to do this, such as Reiki, or you can use the healing symbol (see page 71) in the following exercise:

EXERCISE: HEALING YOUR FOOD

- Draw the healing symbol over the food three times. If you are in a restaurant or public place you can always visualise the symbol.
- Hold your hand open over the food for a moment and visualise light entering your meal.

If I forget to do this before a meal I just sent light down into my stomach and fill myself with it after I have finished eating. This seems to work too, and by sending healing energies directly to your stomach you will also aid the assimilation and digestion of your food. The reason why many of us have weight problems is that our bodies have lost the ability to process the food we eat properly.

Some people believe that raising the vibration of food actually lessens its calorific value. They may well be right and it should certainly take away some of the harmful effects of fat and sugar. Several of my friends claim that they have very successfully lost weight by saying: 'I take from this meal all the nourishment that I need and pass the rest to the world.'

You might like to give it a try and let me know how you get on – it could prove to be the most effective, easiest and cheapest diet yet! However, when I tried it I must admit it didn't work because I felt I had saved some calories and rushed out to get some chocolate to make up.

Where we eat

The location and ambience of a meal are important. The positive energy of the food is enhanced by taking time to prepare the space where we are going to eat it. This also honours those with whom we will share it.

For a special meal at home with the one we love we may opt for candlelight and flowers and gentle music. If we are at work and find ourselves with just a half-hour break and a sandwich to eat, we should at least try to find a quiet spot where we will not be disturbed, away from the demands of our working day. We will be affected by the energy of our work and clutter if we grab a quick bite at a busy desk covered in papers demanding our attention.

Mealtime harmony

As we eat the thoughts and emotions of those present will be passed to our food. The energy in what we eat will be affected by any disharmony or negativity, any anxiety or nervousness. If we are watching television, we will also ingest the negative energy of any violence being shown. It is therefore preferable to eat without watching television or reading a newspaper or even a book. If you are sharing your meal with others try to keep the conversation light and harmonious.

A family meal with all members contributing and sharing the day's events is an uplifting and happy occasion but unfortunately a rarity these days. If you can organise this at least once a week you will definitely feel the benefits.

I have a friend who married into a family of five and then had twins. Every day this large family ate in groups or on the run due to their different schedules and lifestyles. However, every Sunday she insisted on the entire family sitting down together at the table, which was well prepared with cutlery, serviettes, candles and flowers. She said it was hard work for her but well worth it, as it brought the family unit together and everyone found enjoyment not only in the food but also in the company and in the sense of all coming together to share.

It also gave the family the chance to catch up with what everyone else was up to and 'where they were at'. In our house we still have the family Sunday lunch as a way of bringing us all together – even if I almost have to drag some of them away from the football on television.

Medication

Although they aren't 'food' in the usual sense, medicines are taken by mouth with the aim of improving our well-being and so it is worth mentioning them here. I don't intend to start a crusade against modern drugs but I would ask you to check that any medication you are prescribed does in fact suit you and agree with you. I have come across many circumstances where someone is given a drug to cure a problem only to find that their medicine causes further problems and complications in their health.

My own father was given a treatment for high blood pressure – beta blockers – that caused him to suffer from asthma which eventually shortened his life. I am sure you have heard many such stories. If you find that your medication is causing you side effects such as drowsiness, loss of breath, loss of memory or depression I suggest you seek the advice of a complementary healer to try to find a more natural remedy for your problem. Personally I would avoid any drug of any kind whenever possible. Most drugs and medication are toxic, especially if they are taken over a long period.

Hopefully your system will physically reject what it can't take. But do take responsibility for what you put into your body – whether it be a cream cake or a pill.

Food Sensitivities and Allergies

In recent years there has been a marked increase in the number of people who suffer from food sensitivity, intolerance and allergies. I have a problem with wheat, tomatoes, potatoes and refined sugar, among other things. As I am only sensitive to these foods I can have them in small doses without harm, but if you have an allergy it can cause a great deal of discomfort or worse.

A friend of mine and her son are both allergic to cheese, which gives them terrible stomach pains and diarrhoea and has probably been the cause of the boy's early ear problems. They suffer some of the typical symptoms of a food allergy. Other symptoms include bloating, irritable bowel syndrome, extreme indigestion, constipation, skin problems and fatigue.

If you want to check whether you are allergic to certain foods there are now specialist therapists you can turn to. Some of them direct a computer-monitored impulse with the same vibration as the food in question at you, and record your body's reaction. Other therapists use a muscle-response test called kinesiology to detect any intolerance.

Internal congestion caused by tiny stones in the gall bladder, kidneys or liver or by old mucoidal waste in the colon may be the cause of some intolerance. The stones inhibit the healthy functioning of the gall bladder, the kidneys and the liver and the slow production of bile can make it difficult for the stomach and colon to break down food properly, causing discomfort and in some cases a shortage of the important nutrients contained in the food. The way to clear such congestion is to put yourself on a thorough cleansing and detoxification regime.

Detox time

There is no doubt that an excess of refined sugar, refined flour, saturated fat, alcohol, cigarettes and caffeine has a cumulative and detrimental effect on our health. Obviously it is a good idea to keep our intake of all of these to a minimum or at least under control. It is also a good idea to 'detox' from time to time. Not only will this clear your liver, kidneys and colon of the accumulated waste matter of years, but it will also clear away any toxins and negative energy you may have ingested in your food. It will bring release and a clearing away of negativity on an emotional, physical and spiritual level.

If you cleanse yourself physically you will also cleanse yourself mentally and spiritually. This works the other way around too. While I was writing this book I took myself away for two weeks to a place where I wouldn't be disturbed by telephones, e-mails and so on.

While away I ate fairly light food but nothing dramatically different from my normal diet. Yet as I wrote I noticed something strange happening to me. I normally suffer from constipation but found myself rushing to the toilet for the entire time that I was away. Obviously my concentration on the issues of clearing and cleansing and letting go of negativity worked through me at all levels. Of its own accord my body had gone into detox.

As the benefits of detoxing are becoming better known so there are plenty of books being written to help us. One I can recommend is *The Amazing Liver Cleanse Diet* by Andreas Moritz (see Further Reading, page 283). He has found that many illnesses can be cured by thorough cleansing of the liver and kidneys. His book tells us of the dangers of the small stones that can accumulate in our gall bladder, kidneys and liver, with the result that these organs operate less than efficiently, causing our digestion and our entire physical system to become sluggish. This in turn can lead to any number of ailments and, eventually, more serious diseases.

Moritz's cleanse requires abstinence from certain foods and a regime of herbal drinks and apple juice followed by colonic irrigation and a two day 'blitz' of our liver with Epsom salts. The therapist who recommended the book to me has seen remarkable changes in her patients who have used this method.

If you just want to give your liver and kidneys a rest from the overload that they normally take then you could give yourself a month without meat, chicken, caffeine, alcohol, carbonated drinks, chocolate and dairy products. This alone can clear your system of any build-up of toxicity and increase your energy levels. At the back of this book I have suggested several other books on detoxing that you might like to read to help you choose which method suits you best. Whichever process you select – I wish you the best of luck.

Further cleansing

Just drinking water will help to clear you of toxins. We need eight glasses (about two litres) of good water a day to keep our kidneys and general system well flushed and operating efficiently. There are arguments for and against the addition of fluoride to our drinking water but personally I prefer my drinking water untampered with so I buy bottled mineral water. Whatever water you drink, just make sure it is safe by buying it, boiling it or filtering it. And drink plenty of it!

Enemas are an excellent addition to your detox regime. These cleanse the colon with water. You can do them for yourself – you can buy an enema set from a chemist or natural health shop. A more extensive version of an enema is colonic irrigation, where the entire colon is flushed out with water. I have had a course of colonic irrigations and I admit it was not the most pleasant experience of my life, but the results were well worth the slight discomfort of the treatment. The therapist told me that I had an extra kink in my colon, which explained my constipation problem. He also told me to avoid pasta and flour – in fact wheat in all forms.

If you decide to try a colonic irrigation keep your diet light before and after the treatment and avoid alcohol for the week following the treatment as you will be less tolerant to toxins. Only go to an experienced therapist, who should also be able to give you good advice about your diet and what works for you. The therapy is recommended for the prevention of bowel cancer and other common colon disorders, such as constipation. If in doubt check with your doctor.

Energy Foods

To conclude this chapter here is a list of some foods that are both good for you nutritionally and great for raising your energy levels:

- **Vegetables** In particular, broccoli, carrots, spinach, celery and avocado pears (really a fruit) are high in many of the important nutrients and antioxidants that fight toxicity. Onions and garlic are also good for the digestion and are believed to help prevent many conditions, from heart disease to colds.
- **Fruits** All types of fruit are great food and ideal for between-meals snacks instead of sweets or other less healthy foods. Great snacks are dates, bananas and dried fruits, especially apricots – look out for fruit that has been dried naturally without sulphur dioxide. Leave an hour between eating protein meals and fruits, otherwise you may get indigestion as the fruits will become trapped within the slower-digesting protein.
- **Carbohydrates** These include potatoes, rice, bread

and pasta and are good for giving us physical energy. If you have a wheat or gluten allergy you can now buy pasta made from corn starch and rice flour. Choose brown rice as white rice is refined and therefore less beneficial; similarly, wholemeal bread is preferable to white bread made with refined white flour.

- **Oily fish** Salmon, trout and mackerel contain Omega-3 oils that are good for preventing heart disease.

By taking care over the energy that emanates from what we eat and how we eat it, we will nourish and nurture both our body and our spirit. We will now look at how to be aware of other potential sources of negative energy – in our personal belongings and in the places we live in and visit.

5

Negativity in Objects and Places

Negative circumstances, situations and events can all leave their mark on things and places. In this chapter we shall see how personal objects such as jewellery can be affected by the mood and attitudes of the individual who possesses them, and how negative thought forms can leave their imprint on buildings and other aspects of our physical surroundings.

Energy in Objects

My grandmother died before I was born but I have strong connections to her and I feel I know her very well. Over the years my mother has told me many stories about her and her great strength of character. As a young woman she married a successful farmer and they had several very happy years together. They started a family and had two healthy boys and my mother. But then disaster struck.

My grandfather's business partner absconded with all their savings, leaving my grandfather bankrupt and the family close to destitution.

My grandfather was heartbroken at the loss of his beloved farm and my grandmother had to think quickly about how to make a living and find a way to support the family. Times were hard – this was in the 1920s around the time of the Great Depression – and neither of them had obvious skills for employment. However, she was a good cook and managed to secure the lease of a restaurant between London and Brighton.

The venture was a great success mainly due to my grandmother's hard work and determination. Although my family no longer owns it, the restaurant still thrives today.

Examples of energy in jewellery

One of the few possessions that my mother inherited from my grandmother was a golden topaz crystal drop, which she passed on to me when I was in my teens. From that moment I felt close to my grandmother. Whenever I held the drop I felt comforted and in some way protected. I could sense her near me and I soon realised that she was a spirit guide for me.

On one occasion I heard her voice in my head warning me of an accident ahead on the motorway – I moved in to the inside lane just in time. I also heard her telling me when I was about to meet my husband. However, these were isolated incidents and it was a long time before I would communicate with my grandmother properly – in fact it was only about ten years ago, when she came through as an incarnate voice to tell me to start healing. Since then I speak to her quite easily. I also still have her topaz drop and I wear it whenever I want to feel close to her.

This was a positive experience and the topaz drop acted as a bridge between us because the energy of my grandmother's essence was still in the jewellery. If someone with strong psychic sensitivity were to hold it now they would also feel *my* essence and be able to sense things about me. This ability to read clairvoyantly through jewellery or objects that have been close to someone is called psychometry. I once visited a Lebanese fortune-teller who gave me an amazingly accurate psychometric reading just by holding my watch.

If you have a treasured piece of jewellery that has been passed on to you by a member of your family – something that they would often have worn or kept close to them – you will probably feel them near to you by holding and opening yourself to their energies. This can be a truly beautiful experience.

Jewellery will absorb the energies of any traumatic incident or powerful emotional experience – for example, if you are sad for a length of time your possessions will absorb some of this sadness too. Crystals, gemstones, gold and silver will all accept energy quite easily, so if you buy a second-hand piece of jewellery and you are not aware of its origins you may be taking home more than you think. My advice is to cleanse it thoroughly before wearing it yourself. You can use one of a number of methods that I will explain later in this chapter.

It is also possible for the energies of an object to be changed by someone's intentions. Here is an incident that happened to me in my twenties. It is a story of how a beautiful piece of jewellery became contaminated by landing in the wrong hands.

In my late twenties I met a man whom I shall just call Michael. He and I were just friends and dated a few times. He was not a happy man as he had recently split up with his previous girlfriend and in fact he was extremely bitter about the break-up.

Just before this time, my first husband and I had separated. One day I mentioned to Michael that I had decided to have my wedding ring set with precious stones so that I could wear it as a dress ring. I was still fond of my ex-husband and I thought it would make a lovely memento of our time together.

Michael said he had a jeweller friend who could do this for me. It seemed a good idea and I handed him the ring. As soon as I had done this I felt quite sick and thought maybe I had done the wrong thing. I was soon to find out that I had in fact made a big mistake.

Soon after I started to get a series of bad headaches which I blamed on my workload, but they persisted and I became quite exhausted at the end of each day. In fact my energy levels were getting lower and lower day by day. I had no idea what was causing this and soldiered on, hoping that things would get better. Life was generally good for me as I was quite happy and had adapted to my single status. I had an interesting job and was developing a circle of new friends. I didn't see Michael any more because of an incident that I will share later in this book. However, he still had my ring and the only time I contacted him was to remind him to send it back to me.

One night some friends suggested that we join a singles club. It seemed an excellent idea and we all went off to one of the club's presentations at a London hotel. It sounded great fun and the organisers asked those of us who were interested but had not completed an application form to join to stay behind for an interview – I guess to check if we would make suitable members.

When my turn came, the young man who read through my form also passed his hand over it. I realise now that he was a psychic and he was just doing a quick clairvoyant check. He looked up at me and said, 'Are you feeling OK?' I felt a shiver pass through me. 'Not really,' I said. I told him of my headaches and lack of energy. He said that if I was willing I could stay on after the session and he would clear the headaches and generally help me. He seemed trustworthy and genuine so I accepted his offer.

He told me that in his opinion someone was having an adverse effect on me. He thought that the person had dubious intentions and hidden motives. I immediately thought of Michael. I mentioned his name and we both felt our hair stand on end, which is a classic indication that we had touched the energy of dark forces.

He asked me if I had anything of Michael's with me. I opened my bag and we could feel a strong negative energy coming out of it. I emptied it onto the table and the interviewer passed his hands over the contents. He then pulled out two pieces of paper – both were notes that Michael had sent me.

He fetched a tin bowl and burnt the notes – the smell was awful but the atmosphere immediately felt clearer. He then passed his hand over once more and said there was still something else, inside my diary. We looked in and found a page at the back where Michael had written his name and address for me. He tore this out and burnt it too and I started to feel a great deal better.

He then told me to go home and say the Lord's Prayer before going to bed – this would be a form of protection for me. He said that he and his friends would light a candle and pray to help clear Michael's influence upon me. He confirmed that Michael was using my ring to gain energy and strength from me. He also suspected that he was involved in the occult.

I went home without incident and despite a few nerves slept well that night. All the next day I felt fine until 5 o'clock when I was suddenly overcome by extreme tiredness. Later that evening the young man called me and apologised, saying that the candle he had lit for me had gone out at 5 p.m. and he would now use one made of beeswax which hopefully would last longer. After a week of the candle burning and prayers I was freed from the attentions of Michael and cured of my headaches and tiredness.

I didn't hear any more from Michael until a month later, when he unexpectedly called to ask me if I would like to join him at the weekend. He reminded me that it was Hallowe'en and suggested it would be a great idea if we joined up with a group of his friends – to visit their coven! Needless to say, I refused emphatically. A ring is a powerful symbol and is used to show love and attachment – Michael and his associates were clearly perverting this and using it to gain my energy.

Soon after that call the ring arrived in the post, but its energy felt dreadful and I got rid of it as soon as possible. The moral of this story is to be wary of entrusting to anyone else any personal object that you normally keep close to you. If you do, I suggest that after getting it back you cleanse the item by smudging with sage.

Antiques and furniture

Years ago I loved the thought of having enough money to fill my home with antiques. Now, however, I prefer the fresh appeal of something new and I'm less keen on old furniture – though I do have some lovely characterful old pieces that I brought back from China. Like jewellery, antiques can retain energy accumulated from their previous owners, so if you are looking to buy an antique or a second-hand piece of furniture here are a few steps to take to check the item and make sure it doesn't bring with it any negativity from the past:

- To protect yourself, imagine yourself surrounded by a purple flame.
- Stand next to the item and touch it, to make contact.
- Focus on the item, closing your eyes to avoid distraction.
- Allow yourself to open up to the energy of the item and sense any change in your own feelings and emotions.

If you feel anything but positive after following this procedure then don't buy the item. On the other hand, if you do not sense any negative energies in the shop you are very unlikely to feel any at home. The energies of an item won't change when you bring it home – or at least, they certainly won't get any worse. If anything, the atmosphere of your home will uplift them and make the object uniquely yours. If you feel that antiques and furniture that you already own feel negative I suggest that you cleanse them with the smoke of burning sage or incense.

Works of art and handicrafts

Anything that is handmade will hold the mood of the person who created it. This is why we can be so moved by and attracted to some pieces of art. Paintings and sculptures that just cry out to us to be bought possess an appeal that lies both in the combination of colour, form and composition and in the positive energy that the artist has imprinted on the artwork. The actual feelings that he or she was experiencing while creating the work will be captured in the paint, stone or wood. This is why a painting, sculpture or any other handmade item is such a wonderful gift between friends and family. You feel the essence of the person in the gift.

Cleansing your purchases

Whether you buy anything new or second-hand, whether it be an item of jewellery or antique furniture or a kitchen implement, it's generally a good idea to cleanse it before making it part of your home. If the object is of china or glass simply wash it in water containing a drop of juniper essential oil. A larger item can either be sprayed with a room spray made up of water with a little juniper or sage oil, or smudged with sage or incense (sandalwood is good), surrounding and filling the item with the smoke.

Energy in Buildings and Landscapes

Have you ever walked into a house and felt suddenly depressed? If so you will have picked up the negative energies of its past or present occupants. The emotions and moods, thoughts and feelings of people can stay with a building for a very long time. If someone has had an argument in a room just before you enter it you may find yourself sensitive to its energies.

If you view a house you may want to buy you may feel repelled without knowing why, and this could be because the owners have experienced discord or unhappiness. If you are planning to move into a new home check out the atmosphere carefully and find out as much as possible about the previous residents. A building will retain the imprint of traumatic or violent events, leaving it with low vibrations and making the place feel cold and dank. Later in the chapter I will guide you through the steps to take to check the energy of a building.

Of course, buildings can have extremely positive energies too. When I first went to look at our house in Burley I remember being immediately struck by the thought 'This is a happy house.' As I got to know the previous owners better I could see why. They were a lovely family, very close and very happy and totally involved in each other and their beautiful horses. The daughter of the house was a very successful show jumper and so their horses were an intrinsic part of their lives.

The only room of the house that didn't feel so good was the dining room, which they hardly ever used, in fact I think it is where they stored their saddles. They were a 'kitchen family' – everything happened in the big family kitchen, including all their entertaining. This part of the house was particularly inviting and you could feel the friendliness of the place and the owners as soon as you walked through the door.

Energy and building materials

The very fabric of a house or other building will hold the thought forms of its inhabitants. The bricks, the wood, the plaster and especially natural stone will act as conductors and magnets that store the energies of all events and emotions that are played out within the walls.

I've noticed that stone and marble suck in energies more than brick. Wood is a good material for a house as it keeps some of its life and has a calming effect on the energies within. I personally love wooden houses and I think it is a pity that we are not encouraged to build them in Britain. In Finland and Russia it's quite normal to have a house created almost entirely of wood and they are extremely cosy and warm as a result.

Grim events from the past

It is not only buildings that can be affected by the energy of negative emotions or by shocking, violent or traumatic events. The same applies to outdoor locations too. I can remember visiting the battlefield of Spion Kop in South Africa. I don't normally rush to visit such places but my parents were with me on a touring holiday.

Like many men of his generation, my father was interested in war memorials and military history, and my mother was particularly interested in this famous battle because her own father – my grandfather – only avoided being there through an interesting combination of circumstances. He was in the British Army and had applied to become an officer. However, on the very day of the exam he had a blinding headache that was so bad that he failed to complete the test. As a result he resigned from the army. Shortly afterwards his former regiment was sent to South Africa and engaged with the Boers at Spion Kop. The battle was a disaster for the British and the regiment was decimated in one of the worst defeats of its history.

So Spion Kop was a name that meant a lot to our family. We stepped out of the car and walked into the cold, bleak and depressing landscape. I felt shivery and miserable the entire time we were there. You could sense desolation and fear and the horror of the battle was still tangible in the air. It was an awful place and all three of us were pleased to leave.

Memories of dreadful cruelty, pain and anguish of the past will leave their imprints on any place where people have suffered. Although I haven't visited any of the Nazi concentration camps of the Second World War, I am told by those who have that these sites too hold grim and constant reminders of the past – not just in the photographs and the detritus of the ghastly things that happened there, but in the atmosphere in the buildings and in the very air around them.

Not only are you likely to feel the cold and sense the darkness of these places but you may even find that your hair stands on end. This is a sure sign that the lowest of vibrations are present. You may also have sightings of the past event that has left its mark and imprint on the place. You may even hear sounds from the past. These are all energy patterns that are still in place.

An ill-fated building

Some places seem to attract bad luck to their occupants. One day I was taking my mother for a drive around the Cotswolds, a particularly pretty and picturesque part of central England. We had been touring all day and it was getting towards dusk when I was drawn to drive down a windy lane. At the end of the lane we came across a large ruined house. It looked like an old manor house set in an overgrown garden and wood.

We walked around the place for a little while but soon started to feel ill at ease. Dusk was falling and we became completely 'spooked' by the place. It was not only dark and gloomy but seemed sad and desolate too. We hurried back to the car and drove up the lane a short way then stopped to look the house up in our guidebook.

According to the book, one Christmas many years ago, the daughter of the house was celebrating her birthday and the house was filled with party guests. They decided to have a game of hide and seek and she went off to hide. Everyone searched the house high and low but they couldn't find her, and they started to worry. Eventually she was found in an old chest where she had curled up to hide, which had tragically become her coffin. The lid had jammed and she had suffocated and died. A folk-song, *The Mistletoe Bow*, was written about this sad event.

This same house held another similar sad and tragic memory. In the 17th century, during the English Civil War, a servant had hidden the lord of the manor from his enemies in a tiny secret room in the centre of the house. Unfortunately the servant was killed and, since no one else knew his hiding place, the lord too had died.

No wonder the house felt so depressing and dismal, and it was not surprising to learn that it had eventually been left uninhabited and allowed to become a ruin. The energies of one tragic event had helped to foster another – nobody was willing to let fate have a third attempt.

The room at the old inn

Many years ago I had a boyfriend whose mother was the housekeeper of a former inn in Portsmouth in southern England, a wonderful old place on the waterfront in the oldest part of this ancient port. My boyfriend's mother was extremely happy looking after the building, which a large transportation company had bought to entertain its executives and corporate guests.

She only had one problem. The old inn had been beautifully restored and for the most part felt warm and friendly, but there was one room that overlooked the harbour which she had to keep locked up at all times, because every time a dog went into the room it messed in the very centre of the carpet – on exactly the same spot every time. This room, she told me, was where the last fatal duel in England had been fought. The death of one of the duellists had obviously left the room imprinted with the negative energy of the event and this was enough to startle a dog into losing control of itself.

Active Negativity in Places

So far I have concentrated on how past events imprint places and buildings with negativity. We can call this 'inactive' negativity, since its source is no longer active – we can sense the after-effects but we were not present when the negative vibrations were set up, sometime in the past. Let's take a look now at how to deal with situations where we enter places and come into contact with *active* sources of dark and low energy vibrations as they are being created.

Whenever we get close to anything to do with violence, cruelty, pain or abuse of any kind – whether physical, mental or verbal – we will be affected to a greater or lesser degree, depending on how sensitive we are. The places where these things are taking place will also be contaminated. If you have to go to such places because of your work you can be affected even if there is nothing going on when you are there so make sure you use the protection processes that I have described (see page 113) and cleanse yourself thoroughly afterwards.

Active negative energy in cities

Any violence will lower vibrations. I am sure you know parts of your local town or city where you just wouldn't walk at night because you feel threatened. Most large cities have no-go areas, places where you can feel menace and fear. This is often associated with crime or sleaze. If you feel nervous in a part of town then it is often wise to trust your judgement and keep away – your intuition will usually guide you and let you know if you are threatened. Apart from your personal safety you may find that you are considerably affected just by the proximity of such places.

A friend of mine was recently travelling through a part of London. He asked his friend to stop the car so he could buy something from a newsagent. In the short time that it took him to go to the shop and get back to the car he witnessed three criminal and violent situations. He saw a woman break into a car, a fight in an alleyway and a group of young men running from a shop after another incident.

By the time he had returned to the car he felt completely drained. He fell asleep for the next half hour of the journey then asked his friend to stop again as he felt nauseous. At the side of the road he had a short but violent bout of vomiting that left him exhausted. My friend told me that it seemed as if his body was rejecting and cleansing itself of all the negativity he had seen and consequently absorbed. After that he slept all the way home and then went to bed for four hours – his whole being was healing itself from the effects of being in the proximity of violence in the city.

Active negative energy in buildings

So how do you know if there is negative energy in a building? There may be visible physical signs like damp and mould. There will be parts that for no reason seem colder than the rest. The entire place may be colder than its surroundings. A marked temperature drop is always my first clue. You may get goosepimples or shivers even when the heating is on. You may experience the 'cobwebby' feeling that I have already described (see page 31). In extreme cases the hairs on your neck or arms may stand on end.

You may also find that you feel different emotionally – you may suddenly be overcome by sadness or depression, or even feel anxious and fearful. Words like 'dark', 'dismal' and 'depressing' will come to mind when you describe the building itself or particular rooms or areas within it.

Clearing Negative Energies from Buildings and Spaces

There are many things you can do to clear a place of negative energies. Remember, light is stronger than dark and the high vibrations of positive energy will soon overcome those of negativity. All the following methods use high vibrations, whether from a flower essence, a crystal or a sound. I have used them all and they are all effective. Just your intention to lighten up an atmosphere will take you halfway there.

Cleaning

The first thing to do is thoroughly clean the place. Dust and wash the walls and floors and clear away any cobwebs and dirt, especially in corners. Paint or decorate where necessary with light, bright colours. There is more on cleaning out and clearing out a little later in the chapter.

Smudging

Sage is a powerful cleansing herb and when it is dried will burn well, creating lots of smoke. The Native American method called smudging (see page 118) involves waving the smoke from a smouldering bundle of sage twigs into all the corners of the house. Smudge the entire house, including cupboards, lofts, cellars – and every nook and cranny.

Using incense

The smoke from incense sticks can be used for smudging too. They are made with different aromas that are pleasant although sometimes they may be a little intense and overpowering. Incense also comes in block form which can be burnt in a censer, a container that can be swung, distributing the smoke widely into all parts of the house. Priests have used this method to cleanse churches prior to services for hundreds of years. Sandalwood is good for cleansing spaces and lavender will bring a feeling of peace and relaxation.

Using natural room sprays

Natural sprays, rather than the synthetic versions sold in supermarkets, are ideal for cleansing. They come in spray-topped bottles that allow you to spray the building with a fine mist and contain essences of crystals or essential oils (or both) that will clear any negative energies. Some blends are created specifically for cleansing and purifying a room. I always clear my healing room with a room spray before and after each healing session. I also pack a spray when travelling so that I can clear my hotel room.

Burning aromatherapy oils

The most effective way to cleanse a room with aromatherapy oils is to use the sort of aromatherapy burner that is designed to heat a small amount of water containing a few drops of your chosen essential oil. Others heat a few drops of oil alone but if the drops are in water the steam will carry the essence to all parts of a room over a longer period. Oils that are good for clearing include juniper, sage, sandalwood and peppermint. You can also buy blends that are specifically mixed for clearing and cleansing a room.

Playing music

Playing any form of uplifting music will change the atmosphere and raise the energies of a space. Choose something that appeals to you personally, whether it be pop, garage, R&B or classical. Some pieces of classical music seem to have particular healing qualities – for example Gounod's *Ave Maria* and Beethoven's *Pastoral Symphony*.

Chanting

Chanting a mantra is a very effective way of raising the vibrations of a building. Some Buddhist monks do this for a great part of their day – of course each mantra they chant has a different message and a different use. You can buy CDs or tapes of monks chanting mantras to bless and bring down protection for the occupants of a building.

I particularly like to play the mantra *Om Mani Padme Hum*, which is a beautiful blessing that clears negative emotions and attitudes and will change the atmosphere in a room almost instantly. I also have a CD of Gregorian chants, which are an ancient Western version of chanting. You can make up your own mantra to suit yourself and your situation – just make a positive declaration then sing it out loud. The vibration of the words will have a strong uplifting effect not only on the room but on you as well.

Using bells, cymbals and singing bowls

Bells and cymbals emit a wide range of resonances and can quickly affect the space around them. In many mind, body and spirit shops you can buy cymbals like those used by Buddhist monks in their ceremonies. They also use 'singing bowls' that are rubbed with small sticks to create waves of beautifully light vibrations.

Go into all the corners of the house and let the bells, cymbals or bowls ring out, uttering any invocation or affirmation that you may wish for the building as you go. For example, you can invoke the energies of health, prosperity and harmony – the sound of your words will be carried throughout the house by the vibrations of the bells or cymbals.

Using crystal bowls

Another excellent atmosphere cleanser is a crystal bowl. Made from tiny chips of clear quartz crystal, it makes an amazing reverberating sound when rubbed around the rim with a leather-covered baton.

Clapping

Another simple way to clear away stagnant energy that

has accumulated in the nooks and crannies of a building is simply to clap your hands. Just clap several times in the space – you can also utter your invocations or affirmations as you do this.

Using salt

Salt attracts and absorbs negative energies so is a useful substance for house clearing. Either wash down the walls and floors with water containing rock salt, or scatter the dry salt crystals around the edges and into the corners of each room and leave for a day before sweeping up.

Using symbols

Here are two symbols that we have met before which you can also use equally effectively to heal your home or workplace. The release symbol clears away any thought forms and then the healing symbol brings in light and the high-vibration energy of love.

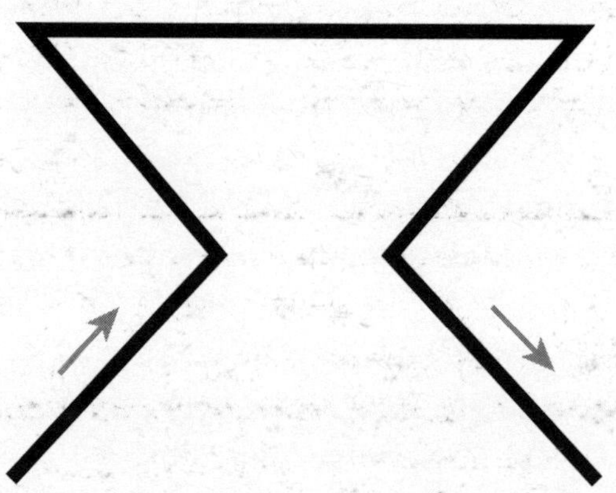

The release symbol.

The healing symbol.

EXERCISE: SPACE CLEARING WITH THE RELEASE SYMBOL AND THE HEALING SYMBOL

- In each corner of every room, draw the release symbol in the air three times. This will clear away any negative energies.
- Now draw the healing symbol three times.
- Hold your palm towards the corner for a few moments and envisage white light pouring from your hand and filling the room.

Blessing

Whenever anyone I know moves into a new home I suggest that either they or I perform a house blessing. Many cultures do this as a matter of course. In the old days in Britain we would hang herbs in the doorway and get a priest to bless a new building. Even now we have ground-breaking and stone-laying ceremonies for large buildings and development projects, and these are a form of blessing. If you are lucky enough to have the opportunity to design and build your own home it is a good idea to bless the ground before you start work.

EXERCISE: BLESSING THE HOUSE

Here is a simple house blessing ceremony that was taught me by my Reiki master some years ago. I believe it has Japanese origins and I know it has a beautiful effect on the energy and atmosphere of everywhere it has been used. Why not do this for your home now?

Stage 1

Place the following items on a tray:

- A flower – to represent life and happiness. Any flower will do although a pink rose, representing love, would be particularly suitable.
- A bowl of water that has been blessed – for blessing the house. If you cannot get hold of any holy water make your own by drawing the healing symbol over the water three times then holding your hand above the water to let the healing energy enter it.
- A small bowl of salt – to represent prosperity.
- A small bowl of uncooked rice – to represent nourishment.
- A lighted candle – to represent light and the divine.
- A lighted stick of incense in a holder – to clear the energies of the house.

Stage 2

Now go to each of the four corners of the house in turn – or you can bless the corners of each room, which I prefer:

- Bow to the corner.
- Draw the healing symbol in the air three times and hold out the palm of your hand to direct the healing energy into the corner.
- Dip the flower on your tray into the blessed water and flick the water into the corner.
- Hold out the tray as if you are symbolically offering its contents to the corner.
- Repeat each of the above stages in each corner.
- Stand in the centre of the room and say out loud: 'I call peace, love, prosperity, good health and happiness into this house' – or use any suitable words of your own. If you are blessing the four corners of the house, speak the words in the centre of the house. I have also performed this ceremony in offices, in which case I have obviously changed the words slightly.
- Draw the harmony symbol (below) in the air three times.

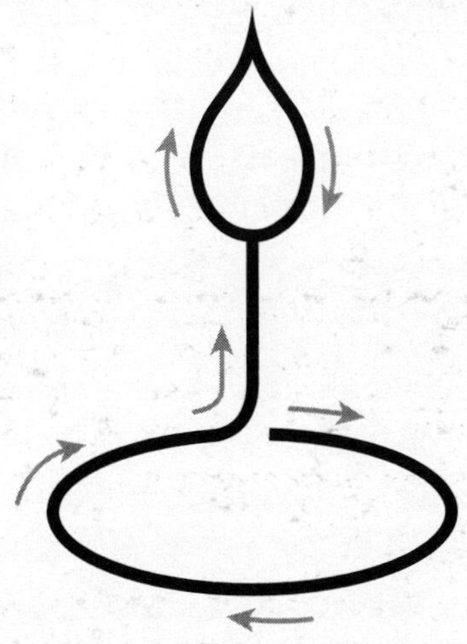

The harmony symbol is used to affirm your blessing of each room.

- Move to the next room and repeat the above stages.

Stage 3

- When you have blessed the entire house, place the tray in the centre of the house (or as near to the centre as you can). Let the incense and candle burn until they go out. You can leave the flower until it fades.

Detoxing Your Home

You don't have to be going through emotional trauma to affect the atmosphere of your house. Negative energies can accumulate in any home. If you allow your house to become messy, overcrowded and cluttered with the detritus of everyday life its energies will become stuck and stale. This in turn will also affect you personally, as your home is a mirror of yourself. Untidy cupboards crammed with things that we never use reflect our state of mind – so let go of the past and move forward!

Spring clean your home, spring clean your life

I often suggest to my patients that they give their homes a 'spring clean' – a thorough clear-out and clean-out – as this shows a symbolic desire to clean out and detox their own lives. By throwing out the leftovers of the past you leave space for new and exciting things to come into the present – whether they be new projects, new opportunities or new people.

I am by nature a squirrel but I have forced myself over the years to have the occasional clear-out and I always feel really good when I've done it. I suggest you apply the principle of keeping only what you love or regularly use. The Victorian poet and artist William Morris said: 'Have nothing in your home which you do not believe to be beautiful or know to be useful.'

If I haven't worn something for a couple of years then it's unlikely that I shall wear it again – it is probably outdated or it was a mistake to have bought it in the first place. You automatically reach into your wardrobe for clothes that you like and that look good on you. If you have clothes that you have never liked or have become bored with, get rid of them. Take them to a charity shop and let someone who does like them have the benefit of them. They certainly aren't helping anyone stuck at the back of your wardrobe – if they cost a lot of money they may even be making you feel guilty.

Give every part of your home a good clean. Vacuum, dust and polish the entire house and make sure you clean the windows; this will ensure that as much light as possible can come in. Clean all the paintwork and give it a new coat of paint if necessary, and check your curtains and furnishings – do you feel they are old, worn and dated? If so buy new ones if you can afford it and choose colours that you truly love, not colours that are 'sensible' and 'go with everything'. Bring light and life into the house with plants.

All this will uplift the energies of your house and help clear away any residue from the past. You won't regret the effort and you will find that you will become more energised and more vibrant as soon as you look around your cleared, cleaned and tidy home. So detox your home and give yourself a spiritual detox at the same time.

You will be amazed by the results of your clear-out and clean-out. One of my clients complained that she felt stuck in life. She was tired and lethargic a lot of the time and was also in desperate need of an increase in her income. She had been in this state for some time so I thought drastic measures were needed. I suggested she detox her house and she set about it straight away.

She found it hard to get started as she lacked the enthusiasm and energy, but as she got underway and cleared away her accumulated clutter she found more and more energy. By the time she had finished clearing and redecorating her house she had acquired a new business contract and the money had started rolling in. She is now living in a spruced-up home and has regained her zest for life – and her prosperity.

Feng Shui – Managing Energy Flow

We have looked at the negative and positive vibrations of energy in a house or other building but we are also affected by the way the energy moves and flows around us. A good 'spring clean' will help to clear any stagnant corners in your home, but let's now look at ways to improve the general energy flow on a constant basis.

The way the energy flows through our houses will affect the way our life flows. If we have areas where the energy is stuck an aspect of our life will mirror this. We will find that we are also blocked in certain ways, or that we are unfocused and scatterbrained – as we have seen, if our house is cluttered and messy so is our mind.

The art of managing the energy in a building or landscape to bring maximum benefit to those who live or work there is called Feng Shui. It originated in China and has been taken by the Chinese to all the parts of the world where they have settled. Nowadays it is widely popular and has also become big business – there are now many companies which rely on a Feng Shui master to help them optimise their success. In Hong Kong no house or office block will be built without the presence of the Feng Shui master to oversee the internal and external design.

In Repulse Bay, where I lived for a time, there is a large apartment building built on a mountainside overlooking the sea. The building was designed with a large hole in the centre in order to allow the energies of the mountain spirit, which the locals call the dragon, to get to the sea. It is believed that the dragon will bring misfortune if he is thwarted in his movement down to the ocean.

My introduction to Feng Shui was in Malaysia. A couple of days after I had moved into our new house we had an exceptionally heavy thunderstorm. The water poured down the street, through the front gates, along the drive and straight into the office at the side of the house. However, when my housekeeper saw this she said, 'Oh, very lucky.' Apparently water pouring into that room meant that a lot of money would come in that way. This was interesting, as I had decided already to use the room to hold computer classes for other expatriate wives. The classes did in fact turn out to be very well attended and were booked up solidly the entire time I gave them.

I know many people who have changed their luck and fortune by moving furniture around and using simple Feng Shui devices. If you are especially interested in Feng Shui, I suggest you read a book by an expert (see Further Reading, page 283). Here are just a few tips and pointers for improving the energy flow of your home that I would recommend from my own personal experience:

The front door

This is the entrance to your home and your interface with

the rest of the world. Keep it as clear and uncluttered as possible and well maintained. Show a shining face! Don't have too many things such as plant pots on your doorstep where you can trip over them. I also suggest you place two Chinese lion statues looking out of your door to bring good luck and to protect you. These are widely available in mind, body and spirit shops.

The entrance hall

A statue or carving facing the door as a sign of welcome is a nice idea. Elephants facing the door are considered lucky. Again keep it clear of clutter and make it as attractive as possible.

The bedroom

Try to avoid having your bed under a window and too close to the door. It is generally accepted that you will relax better if you sleep away from the door and windows and are able to see them clearly from your bed. In psychological terms, this will prevent the unconscious fear that if anyone were to enter your room at night when you are most vulnerable you would have no chance of escaping or defending yourself. However, it is better not to be absolutely facing the bedroom door – again, psychologically, this would enable an intruder to see you before you see them. Your bed should be off the floor to allow the flow of energy to move around and under you.

While we are in the bedroom let's just look at what we keep by the bed. I found that the books, magazines and papers that I kept on my bedside table affected my sleep. I usually have about six books on the go at once; some I am reading, some need to be put away and others are waiting to be read. I also have a pile of interesting articles waiting for me to browse through.

Some nights I felt that my sleep was disturbed and I drifted in and out a lot, so I recently decided to move everything off the bedside table. Since I did so I have found that I sleep far better. The energy of the words and emotions expressed in the books was affecting me – I know it may sound bizarre, but books possess an energy charge from both the author and the subject matter.

You should keep your bedroom clear of anything that breaks the harmony of the room. You want to be peaceful and relaxed in this room, so avoid computers and any office equipment that will bring your focus back to work. What do you want from your bedroom? Whether it be romance, sex, relaxation, just a good night's sleep or all of these you will find that soft lighting, candles, aromatherapy burners, and gentle colours and fabrics are far more conducive than a computer, a television and newspapers.

The toilet and bathroom

If you have an en suite toilet or bathroom always keep the door shut and the toilet seat down. Leaving the toilet seat up invites your money to be flushed away.

General

Sharp points and edges directed into a room are always considered to be bad Feng Shui – the pointed, knife-like energy translates as aggression or opposition in your life. Plants are a good way to shield any corners pointing into a room to soften the impact. If the corner of a neighbouring house is pointing towards your own, put cacti in the window of your house to ward off the aggressive energy.

Prominent heavy beams are also energy blockers. Avoid sitting under them and hang an object on them to break them up visually and psychologically – Feng Shui experts recommend for example a *bagua* symbol (described later in the chapter) or a pair of bamboo flutes. See also the list of objects to enhance your home in the next section. Avoid creating pokey, cluttered corners in your rooms by the way you set out your furniture.

Objects to enhance your home

Here are a few of the objects that you can use to enhance any space and offset any negative aspects:

- **Crystal drops** Hung in a window, these will create prisms of light as the Sun shines through.
- **Fresh flowers** I think one of the most energising and uplifting things you can do for your home is fill it with fresh flowers to bring in life and colour. This is something you can go out and do right now.
- **House plants** Green vegetation and flowers will also bring life, especially to a corner. Choose plants with round leaves that grow upwards – spiky leaves, like sharp corners, are bad Feng Shui.
- **Pictures** Especially those representing joy, happiness and success. These words, written in beautiful Chinese calligraphy, can be bought as framed pictures from mind, body and spirit shops and major stores.
- **Water features** Moving water brings in life and activity.
- **Wind chimes** To create beautiful sounds as they are stirred by the wind.

Your home and your life

Every part of your house represents a different aspect of your life. To find which area relates to which aspect you need to draw an octagonal Feng Shui grid, or *bagua*.

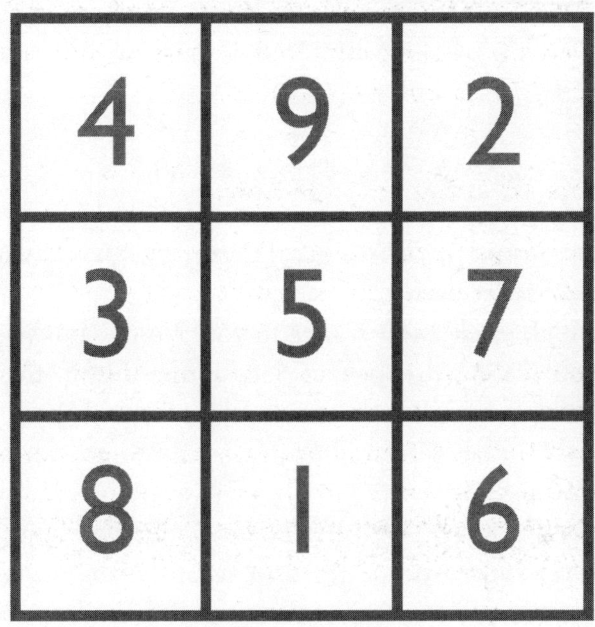

The octagonal bagua symbol is used in Feng Shui *to determine which part of your life is related to each area of your home.*

EXERCISE: RELATING YOUR HOME TO YOUR LIFE WITH THE *BAGUA*

- Draw a plan of your home, apartment or office with the door or entrance that you use most often at the bottom of the plan directly in front of you.

- Divide the plan into eight equal segments. Draw a circle around your plan and divide it into nine equal segments. Your entrance will be in the first segment, at the bottom of the grid.
- Label the entrance '1'. Moving clockwise, number each segment according to Feng Shui practice in the following order: 8, 3, 4, 9, 2, 7, 6. Number 5 is the very centre of the grid.

Here are what the various segments represent.

1. Your career and journey through life, physically and spiritually

If you look after the entrance to your home you will look after your career prospects. Place something in this area that represents success to you, for example a picture of someone you consider to be successful or a flower in full bloom.

8. Contemplation, study and inner knowledge

This part of the house can enhance your inner development, self-knowledge and inner peace. It is therefore a good place to meditate – make sure that it is kept as clear as possible so that you can be at ease with your inner self.

3. Elders and family

This particularly relates to your relationship with your parents and authority.

4. Fortunate blessings, wealth and prosperity

This is an important area of your house as it reflects abundance coming into your life: prosperity, happiness, well-being – all the good things that you want for yourself.

Keep the vibrations up in this segment. An indoor water feature will keep the flow of energy moving, and flowers and plants such as *Crassula argentea* (money tree) will also enhance the space. Place anything that you want to enhance at or above eye level to represent growth, flourishing and positive, uplifting vibes. For example, you could use symbols of prosperity and abundance like a pile of new coins or a painting of a happy person.

Keep the windows clear and clean and let lots of light shine in. Crystals hanging in the window will help to bring spectrums of light into the room. If possible avoid having your toilet in this segment. If it is there then keep the door shut, put a mirror on the outside of the door to reflect away energies, keep the toilet seat down and generally enhance the space as best as you can.

9. Illumination, reputation and fame

This is the segment diametrically opposite your entrance door at the far end of your house. It relates to your spiritual enlightenment and how others regard you. Again, if you seek success, place articles here that represent success to you.

2. Relationships and marriage

To make sure that things are harmonious with your partner keep this part of your house clear and uplifted.

7. Creativity and children

All your creations – whether they be ideas, children, projects or plans – spring from this part of your house. It is here that you can show the world, and acknowledge to yourself, your intention to achieve success in creating all you need.

6. Helpful friends

Make sure that this area of your home is uplifted to ensure that you receive all the help you need. Acknowledge your spirit guides and angels in this corner – maybe with a picture of an angel or a small statue representing your spiritual leader or master.

5. Unity and health

This is the very centre of your house. Keep it clear and fresh as it represents your physical well-being. The cupboard under the stairs often sits in this part of the house. Try to keep it tidy and as uncluttered as possible.

My personal experience

I was interested to discover that I had changed the Feng Shui of my house in Burley without realising it. When we moved in I decided that since we were in the country I would encourage the family to use the side door that leads through a small lobby into our kitchen, rather than having people traipse through the house in wet waterproofs and muddy boots. I went so far as to lock the front door and place a small cupboard in front of it so that everyone would have to enter the house from the side.

By changing the entrance, of course, I had changed the orientation of the eight Feng Shui segments, so the significance of each part of the house would be different for us from what it had been for the previous owners.

Originally the prosperity segment had been a dark and overgrown exterior corner of the house with a toilet on the inside, an area which no one liked and eventually I totally changed. Now, though, it turned out that I had shifted the prosperity segment to the main lounge. Outside this room I had a large pond built with a waterfall that runs down towards that corner of the house. Without realising it, this had also greatly improved the Feng Shui of the house and specifically of our own fortunes. I also put another water feature outside the darker corner of the house, which had now become the segment for contemplation and inner knowledge, and added windows to let in light.

It is certainly true that since we bought the house my husband has gone from strength to strength in his career, which has improved our prosperity, and I suppose my own inner knowledge has come on apace as well.

So I am a great believer in the power of Feng Shui and I pass on what I know to everyone I can. There are many other ways you can use Feng Shui to improve the energy flow of your home and workplace, and there are many good books on the subject. As with all energy work, what you do to your home or office will affect every aspect of your life and you may be surprised at just what turns up for you.

Memorials

I would like to conclude this chapter with a note on how to heal places that have been imprinted with the trauma of a particularly tragic event. I feel that it is important to create something of beauty to offset the horror of the event. One way is to plant a tree or shrub on or near the site of an accident or disaster. This will help to bring life back to the place. A memorial garden is another lovely way to acknowledge and show respect for people who have lost their lives, very often for a good cause. In the case of the Twin Towers in New York, I can think of no better way to help heal the site than creating a beautiful garden that will be an asset to New York and a healing place for those who are grieving.

It is not only the past and present negative energies of people that make their presence felt in our environment. In the following chapter I am going to look at two further environmental sources of energy that are potentially detrimental to our health and well-being – the hazardous electrical energies which surround us in this technological age and the negative energies generated by the Earth itself.

6

Electromagnetic and Earth Energies

We will now look at the ways in which humanity has disturbed the peaceful airwaves around us by creating an onslaught of negative energy in the form of electromagnetic waves. As we shall see, however, there are ways to counteract and live with the hazard of this 'electromagnetic stress'. We will also discover that the Earth itself is not all peace and calm but has its own negative energies that can affect us. Again, once we have looked at the problem of this 'geopathic stress' I will show you ways to protect yourself effectively from harm.

Electromagnetic Stress

This is the name given to the harmful effects of the electromagnetic radiation created by such sources as electricity pylons, substations and power lines, television transmitters and sets, computers, microwave ovens and mobile phones and telecommunications masts – in fact, almost anything that uses or transmits electricity. Some of the articles and scientific studies on this subject make disturbing reading. For example, prolonged exposure to electromagnetic radiation has been linked with the following:

- Leukaemia, brain cancer and other forms of cancer
- ME
- Fatigue and lethargy
- Allergies
- Migraine
- Sinus problems
- Joint pains
- Learning problems
- Memory loss

What upsets me most, though, is the apparent lack of concern on the part of the authorities and the lack of official information that is passed on to the public. It seems that governments are reluctant to show signs of anxiety in case we start to panic, while energy companies are obviously anxious about the detrimental commercial effects. I feel strongly, however, that the public should be given a clearer picture of the potential health hazards of some modern technologies, appliances and sources of power.

One problem is that some people are obviously more sensitive than others to the harmful effects of electromagnetic radiation. Not everyone will get sick even if they are near to the highest voltage outputs. People who already have a low immune system caused by stress, illness, genetic weaknesses, or mental and emotional problems and so on are likely to be more susceptible.

This lack of uniformity makes it difficult for the authorities to draw definite conclusions about who is at risk and in consequence they are reluctant and slow to tell us of the potential dangers. For this reason I think that we should start taking responsibility for our own well-being and that of our families. We can inform ourselves of the hazards of our electricity sources, mobile phones, televisions, computers and so on, and take any necessary steps to counter them. Here are some of the things we could do:

- Join pressure groups and petition for the authorities to stop putting telecommunications masts near schools and homes, to stop building homes near pylons, and to start being more open about the problem to the public.
- Write to our local MP or other elected representative and press him or her to bring the matter to the forefront in parliament.
- Start to take our own precautions to protect ourselves in our own homes, taking what measures we can.
- Work on our own immune systems and health and treat our bodies with respect and care – in other words, make ourselves as strong as we can be.

Let's take a closer look at the chief causes of electromagnetic radiation and what we can do either to neutralise the effects or to protect ourselves.

Major sources

The radiation from electricity pylons, power stations and substations, overhead and underground power lines, and radio masts is far too powerful to be neutralised. All I suggest is that you avoid them. Don't buy a house if it is close to a pylon or mast, and oppose any plans to put any of these structures in local populated areas, especially near homes and schools.

Televisions

Collectively our televisions emit a lot of radiation into the atmosphere. However, an individual set is only likely to cause harm to someone who sits really close to it for long periods. As children appear to be particularly susceptible to the problems of electromagnetic stress I suggest that you make sure they watch television from a sensible distance, at least five feet away.

Turn the television off when it's not in use and don't leave it in standby mode – a recent study showed that all the sets left on standby in Britain emit as much electricity and electromagnetic radiation as a small city. I would especially recommend that you do not have a television in your bedroom.

Computers

To those of you who spend hours at the computer either for work or entertainment I suggest you buy some crystals to absorb the negative energies they emit. I put obsidian, tourmaline and a clear quartz crystal called an apophyllite crystal tip on my computer. Apophyllites, which belong to the zeolite crystal family and are found in central India, are particularly effective against the harmful emissions from televisions, computers and other electrical appliances.

Ask at your local mind, body and spirit shop for these and any other crystals or devices that they recommend for this purpose. Remember to clean the crystals frequently otherwise they will lose their effectiveness. Try to moderate your use of the computer at home and turn it off when you're not using it. As with a television, try to avoid having a computer in the bedroom. If you cannot bear to be apart from it for long or don't have room elsewhere, put up a screen of some kind between the computer and your bed.

Mobile phones

As I am writing this book growing concern is being expressed in the media about the dangers of mobile phones, especially for children and young people. There is some evidence to suggest that people who use a mobile phone for prolonged periods may have a greater than normal chance of suffering from brain tumours and brain damage. One study even claims that the radiation from mobiles may adversely affect the ability of white blood cells to combat disease.

Mobiles certainly cause some people headaches, nausea, memory loss and mental stress. It seems they are just as hazardous when they are on standby. In this case men are more likely to be affected than women, who tend to keep their phones in a bag and not in a pocket or on a belt – harmful radiation may penetrate any part of the body, not just the head. Ironically, the radiation emitted decreases the closer the mobile phone is to a phone mast – it will emit more when it is straining to find a signal from a mast that is some distance away.

To help avoid any problems I suggest that you keep your use to a minimum and use 'hands-free' devices when you can. I have attached a device to my mobile phone called an Ecoflow Vector 100, which neutralises the harmful electromagnetic radiation from both mobile phones and cordless phones.

Electric power points

The electrical wiring, switches and sockets that we all have in our homes are comparatively harmless unless you sleep with a socket close to your head. However, some people are sensitive to even this form of electric field and in Britain the ring main method of distributing electricity around the house means that we are surrounded by electricity.

In their book *Healing Sick Houses* (see Further Reading, page 283), Ron and Ann Proctor tell a story of a woman who became very sick from the effects of the electricity supply in her house. Her husband eventually solved the problem by placing a crystal cluster on the fuse box. You can also neutralise electric power points by covering them with household foil.

Fluorescent lighting

This form of electric light gives off more pollution than a normal light bulb, as do the new long-life bulbs. Avoid using these lights in your home, particularly in a room where you will be spending any length of time.

Clock radios

These innocuous-looking devices are more hazardous than you think – they emit a powerful electromagnetic field right by our heads while we lie sleeping. My advice is to go back to an old-fashioned mechanical alarm clock. I have banned electric clocks in our house. This is an easy precaution for you to take and will cause very little inconvenience.

Microwaves

Microwaves transmitted through the atmosphere are a menace but the only way to protect yourself from harm is to avoid living near masts and transmitters. The microwave cookers in our homes are relatively harmless as long as you don't sit or stand right next to them while they are in use.

General precautions

It seems that if we are moving around and in and out of an electromagnetic radiation field then it poses little threat to our health. We are most at risk if we spend considerable periods within a radiation field, for example sitting in one place for a length of time or lying in bed asleep. Therefore take particular care in your bedrooms and where you sit most evenings, by covering plug sockets with aluminium foil and turning off any electrical devices when not in use.

If you are concerned and think that you may be affected by local power cables, pylons and so on, or you just want to check the levels in your home, you can call a specialist to come and measure the voltage and emissions in and around your building. There are also companies that will detect and measure the electronic pollution and electromagnetic fields.

Air Pollution

Electrical equipment in our homes and offices is also responsible for contaminating the air we breathe. The atmosphere around us contains positive and negative ions, electrically charged molecules which make up the air. Basically, without getting too technical, oxygen consists of negative ions and nitrogen of positive ones.

There needs to be a correct balance of positive and negative ions for the air to be supportive for us. If the negative ions become depleted in any way we will be breathing in less oxygen. When we have less oxygen in our blood we will not only think less clearly but may also experience breathing difficulties and other problems. Typical symptoms for someone breathing in air that is low in negative ions are:

- Asthma
- Bronchitis
- Depression and anxiety
- Dizziness
- Hay fever
- Headaches
- High blood pressure
- Lowered physical and mental functioning
- Sinus problems
- Skin rashes

A major cause – static electricity

Certain air pollutants deplete and 'smother' the negative ions, lowering the levels of oxygen. Among the most common pollutants are aerosols, dust and dust mites, factory emissions, smoke and exhaust fumes. However, another of the main causes of negative ion depletion is static electricity. Static occurs naturally, for example during thunderstorms, but nowadays there are also many sources that are of human origin. As anyone who has had a static shock in a room with nylon carpets will know, certain fabrics will cause static. But in this modern age the major sources of static in our lives are electrical equipment, especially air conditioning and computer and television screens.

The static charges that build up on a computer VDU or a television screen attract and neutralise any surrounding negative ions, creating a zone of ion depletion. This is especially hazardous for people who spend a long time at a computer, who may suffer what has been called 'Video Operator's Distress Syndrome' (VODS). Its symptoms may include headaches, dizziness, fatigue, rashes and breathing problems. Also the ion imbalance attracts dust and other airborne pollutants to the screen and the person using it.

Counteracting negative ion depletion

So what can we do to deal with the problems of oxygen depletion in general and VODS in particular? To begin with, we can increase our intake of oxygen in the following ways.

Spend time in nature

Trees, plants and flowers spend their entire existence creating oxygen – make the most of them and spend as much time as possible outdoors enjoying nature. You could also fill your homes and offices with plants and flowers. Not only will this make your surroundings more attractive and visually uplifting but it will also help your breathing problems. (Of course, watch out for heavy pollen producers such as grasses as these can affect hay fever sufferers.)

Drink more water

This is a great source of oxygen. Drink lots of it, preferably mineral water or filtered tap water. I have put a water cooler in my kitchen to tempt me to drink more water. It wasn't expensive and I buy mineral water from the supermarket in large containers to bring the cost down. Since we've had this installed the whole family has drunk much more water because it's so easily available. You can also buy oxygen supplements that you can add to your water to increase the amount of oxygen in your system.

Take more exercise

Regular exercise will improve your blood circulation, which will make your lungs more efficient at absorbing oxygen and distributing it through your blood to your entire body. Outdoor exercise, especially in green spaces or the countryside, where oxygen is least depleted, will obviously be even more beneficial than exercise taken in an enclosed space like a gym. When the weather is good and when I feel enthusiastic I take a walk or jog through the woods where I live. I always feel far better (after I've recovered) than when I've used the running machine at the gym.

Use an ioniser

There are products on the market now that actually produce negative ions. Studies indicate that these can very effectively reduce the symptoms suffered by computer users in particular. Another useful device is an ionising mat that sends a stream of negative ions into a drink placed on it. You can also place the mat under food to slow down deterioration and the creation of mould.

Negative Energies from Technology – Your Personal Approach

I mentioned earlier that one of the problems with the analysis of the results of scientific research into electromagnetic stress is that not everybody will be affected by the problem even if they live in the same conditions, such as close to pylons or substations. Why do some people get sick when others do not? Here are some of the reasons why you may be more susceptible to the harmful effects of electromagnetic stress:

- **Genetic factors** Your family may have a history of cancer, so you may be more likely to contract this form of illness.
- **Lowered immunity** You may be run down or your immune system may be lowered due to illness, emotional upsets or stress.
- **Negative outlook** You may be depressed or negative in your thinking and attitude. You may even 'expect' to get sick. You are fearful and anxious about your health and your future.

What can you do?

There is little you can do about inherited susceptibilities but you can do a lot about the second two points. By taking the initiative and deciding that you will make yourself as physically, mentally and emotionally strong as you can you will be limiting your chances of becoming a victim of these environmental risks. You can address as many problems as possible by following some of my suggestions and reading books and informed articles to find out the latest thinking, products and supplements that are available to combat the dangers. You can also endeavour to take a positive and upbeat attitude to life in general:

- Look for the good in everything and everyone.
- See and acknowledge the blessings in your life rather than bemoan the things that you lack.
- Enjoy life – take your time and stop to 'smell the roses'.
- Look after your health – eat well and take regular exercise.

As a species the human race has managed to adapt itself to many environmental changes and threats throughout the thousands of years of its existence. There is no reason why we shouldn't adapt again. Our bodies will become stronger in fighting the new threats around us and our genes will become modified to handle the environment and new dangers that we have to combat. For example, scientists have found that many of us have a gene that will allow us to fight off the bubonic plague that destroyed so many lives in the Middle Ages of Europe. People with this gene also seem to be immune to the HIV virus, so we can adapt and modify our immune system to withstand new health hazards.

We can also use our intelligence to produce countermeasures – which we are now doing. There has always been an antidote for all health problems – it's just for us to find it. Finally and most importantly, we can use our free will to decide for ourselves what is good for us as individuals – and we can take responsibility for our own health.

A positive note

I'd like to end this section on the negative effects of modern technology on an upbeat note. First of all, let's remind ourselves of all the advantages that those technological developments brought us. Computers and laser technology used in surgery have saved many lives, as have X-rays and other electronic diagnostic machines. They are polluting our atmosphere with electromagnetic and other forms of radiation but they are also doing us a lot of good. Don't make them into ogres – you will then be affected not only by the emissions but also by your fear of them.

Remember that the energy of your fears will create a negative thought form that will only enhance the negative effects of the emissions. Ironically, even electromagnetic fields are now being used for healing, with magnotherapy products that help arthritis, poor circulation, migraines, insomnia, blood pressure and many more health problems.

With a positive and sensible attitude to the latest technological advances we can get the best from them and still live happy and healthy lives. I will leave this subject now with a reminder of some other sources of positive and uplifting vibrations, the very best of medicine and the best protection from all forms of negativity:

- Joy and laughter
- Love
- Mutually loving and fulfilling sex
- Universal energies – brought to you by the healing symbol
- Light
- Music

- The beauty of nature
- Good food

Negative Earth Energies

We will now look at the potentially harmful negative energy that is created by the planet Earth itself. The Earth is a living being and therefore has an energy field. It suffers from stress and energy distortions just as we do and there are places where the Earth's energies have become stagnant and blocked. The disturbance caused by such misaligned and distorted energies is called geopathic stress.

What causes geopathic stress? Sometimes it is created by natural causes such as seismic fault lines, cracks or lesions where the Earth's crust is weak and under great tension. This tension leads to volcanic eruptions, earthquakes and earth tremors. Other sources are cliffs that collapse from sea erosion and subsidence from underwater streams. However, we humans have also created problems through our lack of consideration for the environment.

Every time we build a dam or a power station, sink a mine or excavate a quarry, dump toxic waste into a river, pollute the sea or create a landfill site we cause problems. Housing and road developments affect the natural flow of Earth energy. The sickness of the Earth can then affect us. Let's look at some of the situations that can occur.

Earth energy lines

Just as we have meridians through which energy flows through and around our body and aura, the Earth has its own energy lines performing the same task. These lines form grids around the Earth's surface. The lines of the Hartmann Grid run from north to south and east to west. Those of the Currie Grid run diagonally. Birds use these lines to guide them on their migrations and animals use them to find their way to water and to their favourite grazing and hunting places.

Ley lines

Some of these energy lines are of major significance – they are like the motorways of the Earth energy world. Known as ley lines, they are powerful and have great influence on the natural world and ourselves. Where ley lines cross each other the positive energies become magnified, setting up a very high vibration that can create a very special spiritual environment.

The result, especially when the lines are powerful, is a rarefied atmosphere. Where the air is rare – light – it is easier to make contact with other dimensions, with the etheric realm and the higher levels of the spirit world. We can also get closer to God. That is why the junctions of powerful positive ley lines have often been chosen for worship and are marked by sacred sites.

One of the best known of these major lines in England is the 'Michael and Mary' line. It starts in the south-west in Cornwall and travels all the way across the country to Norfolk in the east. All along this line there are churches and other sites of ancient places of worship. Many of the churches are named in honour of St Michael or the Virgin Mary, hence the name of the ley line. Another line runs through the prehistoric sites of Avebury and Stonehenge and also the soaring medieval Gothic cathedral of Salisbury, all of which are extraordinary places of wonderful spiritual energy.

Because of the draw of these special locations it is not unusual to find that Christian churches have been built on earlier sacred sites. Our ancient ancestors were clearly sensitive to these Earth energies and could intuitively sense where to build their places of worship. This is probably because they lived much closer to nature than we do now. Of course, our minds are distracted by so many things these days and we no longer spend all our waking hours concerned with hunting or growing food and just surviving. Our modern lifestyle and technologies mean we are involved not just in the concerns of our family, village and local community, but in what is happening nationally and globally too.

In other words, we take an interest in a far wider environment than our ancestors did – but ironically it means that we have lost their intimacy with nature. Our ancestors were completely in tune with their habitat. They knew every rock, stream, valley and tree in their immediate locality. Everything had its own energy, its own spirit, and therefore they were far more spiritually influenced when they chose their sites for homes and worship. These days we are influenced by proximity to roads, railway stations, the availability of free land and, of course, financial considerations.

Negative energy lines

In early times Earth energy lines were universally positively charged and were beneficial to all. Water that flowed over them picked up this positivity and spread high vibration energy across the land. However, over time some lines of energy have become distorted either wholly or in part and their polarity has changed from positive to negative. In most cases, unsurprisingly, the change has been caused by human beings. As we have already seen, any negative event will change the energies of a place. Major traumas or physical changes to the natural existing lie of the land will upset the natural ecology and therefore the flow of the energy lines. Here are just a few of the common human sources of disruption to the Earth's energies:

- Mines, quarries and oil or gas rigs.
- Roads and motorways.
- Dams, waterworks and the redirection of rivers.
- Power stations, pylons, microwave masts and transmitters.
- Overhead and underground power cables.
- Large construction sites – shopping precincts, office blocks, factories, housing estates.
- Tunnels and underpasses.
- Accidents – plane crashes, road accidents.
- Explosions – bombs, detonations.
- Sites of human cruelty and misery – concentration camps, torture chambers, prisons, workhouses, orphanages.
- Sites of greed and exploitation – the factories of the past, office blocks of businesses which deliberately exploit humanity or the environment, such as sweatshops and mining or logging companies.
- Cemeteries and crematoria – owing to the fear so many people have of death and the grief that is expressed in these places.
- Hospitals.
- Sites of black magic and other harmful occult practices.
- Sites of mass killing such as battlefields.
- The presence of spirit activity (ghosts).

Any of these can turn the helpful and positive energy of a line into a negative one. If one of these negative lines – especially one of any great power – runs through your property you will be affected in some way. The extent of the effect will depend upon your sensitivity and on the state of your mind, emotions and physical health.

Crossed negative lines

If two powerful ley lines that have turned negative cross then we have a change in atmosphere. Instead of connecting to the positive, to the light of the spirit world, to enlightenment and to the divine, the site will be under opposite influences. It will be open to the darker aspects of the spirit world. The energy will be dark and the vibrations low. This energy will attract lost spirits of those who have passed over, especially if they are angry – we shall be looking at these in the next chapter. The location will also attract those of the living who wallow in these darker energies – practitioners of black magic and other dark arts.

Water as an energy carrier

Water has a 'memory' – the particles that make up water have energy fields that can absorb energy and carry it from one place to another. In other words if a stream or river runs through or across land that has become seriously contaminated by negative energy then the entire river and stream may be contaminated in turn. If the water were then to run through your land or under your house – don't forget there are many underground watercourses – this energy would affect you too.

The Effects of Negative Earth Energy

Any of us can be affected whenever we visit a place prone to by geopathic stress, whether it be workplace, hospital, school, shopping centre or public offices. However, remember that everyone has different levels of sensitivity so the energies will not affect everyone in the same way. The effects may be manifested in a number of ways:

Your personal life:

- Lack of energy.
- Depression or low spirits.
- 'Bad luck syndrome' – the occupants of a building may experience a general lack of prosperity, lack of advancement at work, limited fortunes, and a sense that they are getting all the bad breaks and none of the good ones, despite every attempt to be positive.
- Lowered immunity – do you seem to catch every virus and germ that is going around?
- General malaise and sickness – or even serious illness.
- Insomnia.
- Unhappiness and sadness without obvious cause.
- Anxiety – even panic attacks.
- Irritability.
- Disharmony and friction among those who share a building, whether family or colleagues.

Your home or place of work:

- Difficult to heat and make cosy.
- Feels dark and uninviting.
- Some areas or rooms seem cooler and less inviting than others.
- Decoration doesn't last, and is prone to mould and discolouring on both the interior and the exterior.

- Problems with the utility supplies – gas, water, electricity, phones.
- 'Sick building syndrome' – the people within the building find it difficult to function well and often suffer fatigue and sickness themselves.

The land around you:

- Flowers don't grow as well as they should in some parts of the garden.
- Certain trees and shrubs die or won't produce good flowers or fruits as they should.
- Moss proliferates.

Detecting Negative Energy Lines

If you suspect that geopathic stress may be affecting your home or workplace there are a number of ways of identifying its source. Here are some of the most effective methods.

Dowsing

The most time-honoured way of finding negative energies in buildings is called dowsing. I have always been fascinated by this system for investigating the unseen and I wonder if it was a coincidence that my maiden name was Dowse! Dowsing is the use of a divining tool to find something that cannot be detected by our senses of hearing, sight, smell or touch.

There are various different methods of dowsing using a variety of tools, such as dowsing rods or a pendulum. The process has been around for centuries and has proved remarkably successful – it has been used to discover underground reserves of water and oil, gold and precious minerals of all kinds, archaeological remains, lost possessions and, of course, ley lines. In fact you can dowse for pretty much anything. I have even used dowsing to detect whether patients have food and drink allergies or sensitivities and vitamin deficiencies.

When I lived in Kuala Lumpur in Malaysia I had a mischievous spirit in our house. She once hid an unusual diamond ring of mine that I wore quite often. One day I realised that I hadn't seen this ring for some time. I searched the house from top to bottom – I looked in all the likely places that the ring could have been, but without success.

I then decided to use my pendulum, which is my preferred dowsing tool. I drew a map of the house and by a process of elimination detected that the ring was in the top cupboard of my wardrobe, which I needed a chair to reach. I eventually found the ring at the back of the cupboard in an old handbag which I hadn't used since arriving at the house. Unless I had dowsed with my pendulum there is no chance that I would have found that ring for years, or at least until my next clear-out.

Divining rods

The traditional dowsing tools used for centuries in Europe are Y-shaped divining rods. These are typically cut from a hazel tree, but apple and willow are also very popular – in fact twigs from any tree can be used as long as they are pliable. You can also use plastic or metal, or even adapt a coat hanger. I dowsed my entire garden with a workshop group one day and we all used coat hangers very successfully. You need to make or cut your rods into a Y-shape. To divine you hold them with your palms up and the tip of the Y towards you. This is a good tool for detecting Earth energies or anything hidden underground.

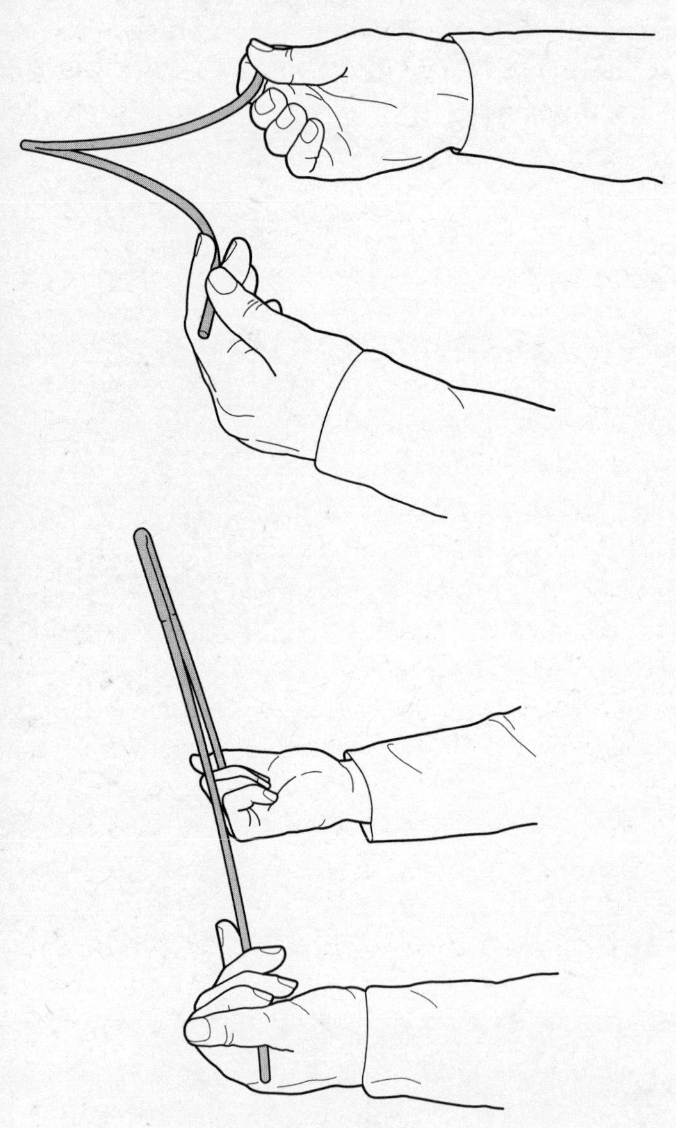

Y-shaped divining rod.

A pair of L-shaped divining rods is also highly effective and easy to use. You can buy these in most New Age or mind, body and spirit shops. They are made of metal and are normally about a foot long. Each rod has a handle at right angles that is held within a sheath that allows the rod to move and change direction easily when you hold it during dowsing.

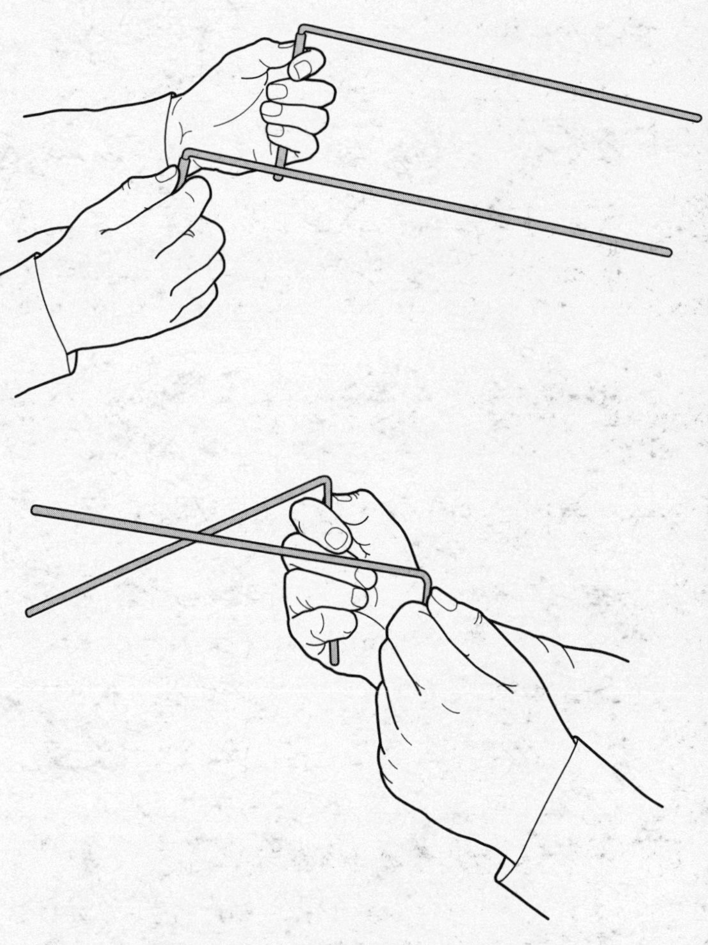

L-shaped divining rods.

Exercise: Dowsing for Negative Earth Energies with Divining Rods

- Close your eyes and inhale deeply four times to help you to relax and focus.
- Envisage yourself surrounded by a protective purple flame or white light. You should protect yourself because you are moving into an altered state of consciousness and will be connecting specifically with negative energies.
- Focus constantly on what you are looking for. Try to keep your mind blank – try not to let it get in the way by thinking logically where power lines might be. If this is difficult it may be helpful to think of a candle flame or something neutral like a flower.
- Hold your divining rod or rods in front of you reasonably firmly. Both types should be parallel to the ground. The L-shaped rods should also be parallel to one another.
- Open your eyes and walk slowly over the area that you are dowsing. The rods will move in response to a source of energy. The L-shaped rods will either spin away from one another or, most often, will cross. A Y-shaped rod will either dip or rise.

When you are practising dowsing you could try looking for the normal lower-powered lines that make up the Hartmann and Currie grids. Think of positive grid lines when you search – these are quite close together and therefore you will get a quick response to your dowsing. Then you can move on to divine for the high-powered ley lines.

The pendulum

My preferred dowsing tool is a pendulum. This can be any weighted object hanging from a chain, thread or string. For a long time I used my grandmother's topaz drop. Now I have a pink rose quartz on a silver chain that was made specifically as a pendulum. You can use the pendulum in any location and you can dowse with it in much the same way as you would use the divining rods.

Before you start, though, I think it's a good idea to establish a few facts with your pendulum as you can get more information from this than you can with the rods – you can 'speak' to your pendulum and ask it questions. It will generally give a 'yes' or 'no' answer and mine goes around in a circle for 'maybe' and 'sometimes', or if my question is not specific enough for it to give a precise response.

I had a friend who could get a number of different responses from her pendulum and between them they had an entire vocabulary. However, mostly you will have to work with 'yes', 'no' and 'maybe'.

Exercise: Detecting Negative Earth Energies Using Your Pendulum

Stage 1

- Hold the thread or chain of your pendulum between your thumb and index finger or loop it over your index finger.
- Allow about six inches of chain to hang down.
- Find out which way the pendulum swings to indicate 'yes' by asking questions to which you already know the answer, for example: 'Is my name . . . ?', 'Do I live

in . . . ?', 'Was I born on . . . ?' and so on. Keep the pendulum as still as possible and concentrate on the question you are asking. The pendulum should swing of its own accord in response.

- Double-check by asking questions to which you know the answer is 'no'. The pendulum should swing in the opposite direction. Remember only to ask very precise questions. When you have established which direction indicates which response you are ready to begin dowsing.

Stage 2

- Close your eyes and inhale deeply to quieten yourself and your mind.
- Protect yourself by putting yourself in your egg, or imagine yourself surrounded by a purple flame or white light.
- Open your eyes and with your question in mind start to walk over the selected area, holding your pendulum as steady as you can in front of you.
- As you walk, ask clear questions such as: 'Am I getting near to a negative energy line?', 'Is this the centre of a grid line?', 'Is this a negative line I am standing in now?', and so on.

Once you have found your negative lines or underground watercourse – or whatever it is you are searching for – mark the spot.

Dowsing at a distance

Personally I prefer to do my energy-dowsing work on houses from a distance. Apart from the time this saves in travelling to the house and back, I feel that on site I am more likely to be distracted and to make assumptions that could falsify my pendulum results. For example, if I walked into a room that felt a little chilly, my logical mind might immediately generate the thought 'there's a negative area or negative line in here' – before I have even checked by dowsing with my pendulum.

This thought could interfere with my attempt to clear my mind during the dowsing process. The room could simply be cold because it isn't much used and the heating has been turned off, or there could be some short-term negativity of human origin in the room because of a recent argument. If you are looking for geopathic stress you are trying to detect more serious, long-term energy distortions.

I prefer to do my dowsing, and even a lot of the remedial healing that might be required, from a distance. Let's look at how this works.

Exercise: Distance Dowsing with the Pendulum

Stage 1

- Make a plan of the building that you are checking on a clean piece of paper. I suggest that you don't use recycled paper or a sheet that has any other writing on it as your pendulum may pick up spurious information from this. If you are doing this for someone else get them to send you the plan of their house, marking the main entrance, all the rooms and the windows. They should provide a plan of each floor and include any outbuilding, garages and conservatories. You can also dowse your own home from a plan, even though you have access to the real thing.

Stage 2

- Take your pendulum, relax and protect yourself as described in the previous exercise.
- Ask your pendulum if it is a good time to conduct your investigation.
- If the answer is 'yes', ask if there are any negative energies affecting the house and its occupants.
- If the answer is 'yes', ask if there are any negative energies created by electromagnetic stress.
- If the answer is 'yes', ask if you can heal these energies.
- Ask if there any negative energies created by geopathic stress.
- If the answer is 'yes', ask if there are any underground streams causing problems.
- If the answer is 'yes', ask if you can heal these energies.
- Ask if there are any negative Earth energy lines causing problems.
- If the answer is 'yes', ask if you can heal these energies.
- Ask how many of these lines there are ('Is there one line?' 'Are there two lines?').
- If there is more than one negative line, ask if they cross.
- If the answer is 'yes', ask if you can heal this powerful source of negative energy.

Stage 3

- Now place the middle or index finger of your free hand on the outside border of your house plan – the outer walls.

- Slowly move your finger around the border, asking the pendulum: 'Is this the entry point of an energy line?'
- When you get a strong 'yes' answer put a cross on the plan at that point.
- Continue in the same manner, looking for the exit point of the line.
- Do this for every line and note where any lines cross on your plan. The place where energy lines cross is the most negative point. If it passes through a bed (they affect up to a considerable height, so check upstairs as well as down) or a favourite chair then you most likely will find that the person who occupies that spot will have been affected by geopathic stress.

A girlfriend of mine in Malaysia, let me call her Sue, had been complaining for a couple of years about her partner's problems. He had been having trouble with his business and with his emotional life. Recently he had complained of always feeling tired and he was niggardly and irritable a lot of the time. I asked Sue if there had been any changes in the environment around her home at the time these problems began. She said that there had been a major office development very close by. Their house used to have an outlook over a tropical forest but now overlooked this new complex.

I asked Sue to carry out the exercise that I have just described. She called me back a few hours later, very excited. She had found two negative energy lines crossing right through their bed – on her husband's side. The negative lines were probably caused by the new development close to their home. She has now put into effect a healing process which I will look at a little later in the chapter. They felt immediate relief.

Animals as energy detectors

All animals are sensitive to energies and particularly Earth energies. They are more in tune with nature generally than us and can be great barometers of the level and power of energies around you. Next time you go past animals grazing in a field that has a pylon in it check where the animals are lying and sleeping – you will find that they will get away as far possible from the source of negativity.

Most animals will automatically go to the location of the best energy they can find. Your dog will intuitively seek out any 'hot spots' of good energy and make them its favourite sleeping places. (My two dogs have found the positive ley line that goes through our house. When my dog Prince was ill recently he left my side and went to lie right on the line, in the centre of the house where it is at its strongest. After he died our other dog, Sophie, spent all her time lying on the line facing the incoming energy, as though she was using it as a source of healing for her loss.)

Cats, on the other hand, prefer to sit on negative energy spots. I don't know why they do this, but perhaps they are mopping up the low energies for their owners. Whatever the reason, if you have a cat you will definitely be able to identify the lower energy areas of your home – just study where your pet likes to take its naps.

How to Heal Negative Earth Energies

I am now going to show you how to deal with negative energy lines and clear buildings, especially at points where lines cross. Here is what I suggested to my friend Sue. For this exercise you will need the following:

- Four clear quartz crystals called 'terminators'. These are long, thin crystals with a point on at least one end. They need only be about 1 inch/2.5 cm long.
- One clear quartz cluster. This is, as it sounds, a cluster of terminators on a bed of crystal. The points tend to stick out in all directions. A small one will suffice.
- A natural room spray.

Exercise: Earth Energy Healing

Stage 1

- First of all cleanse the crystals in salt water overnight. Use natural rock salt and spring or mineral water or, if you can, sea water.
- Charge the crystals by leaving them outside for a further 24 hours in natural light. Bright sunlight and moonlight are ideal, but rain is also good – better still if there is a thunderstorm.

Stage 2

- Take the crystals in your hands and visualise them filled with light.
- 'Programme' the crystals by saying: 'I fill you with love and light and charge you with bringing joy, love, peace, harmony and prosperity to this home [or office or workplace].'
- At the entry and exit points of the negative energy lines, pierce the ground outside the house with a terminator crystal. If you live in an apartment or a linked house (a terrace or semi-detached) simply place the terminator at the appropriate point within the house. I sometimes use BluTack to hold a crystal in place on a skirting board or in a cupboard.

- If possible place the quartz cluster at the point of any crossed energies, or as near to it as you can. My friend Sue was fortunate because she was able to place hers under the bed. You could place a crystal on each floor at the same point but this is not really necessary.
- Now stand close to but not on the energy line and envisage it being turned into bright white light.
- Draw the healing symbol in the air and hold your palms out in both directions, sending healing energies from your hands along the length of the line. Repeat for all the negative lines that go through the building.
- Spray the entire house with the room spray – including in every cupboard, under all the beds and in the loft, basement and cellar. The house will now be clear of negative Earth energies.

I suggested that you stand near but not on the energy lines while you are clearing them. This is because they may affect you as you open up to them in acknowledging their existence. Sue and a friend who helped her with her house healing both felt very nauseous and dizzy while they were doing the checking. When the crystals were put into the ground their nausea and dizziness immediately cleared and they felt better. People have even been known to be sick by getting too close to the energies. I have experienced a muzzy head – but this always goes once I have performed the healing.

This healing exercise may have immediate benefits – I did a clearing recently and the owner and I both instantly felt a complete change in the energy and atmosphere of the house. In other cases it may be some time before you see a difference in the health and well-being of everyone in the house. After you have performed the healing I suggest that you complete the cleansing of the house with a house-blessing (see page 169).

The Moon

I cannot leave this chapter about the effects of Earth energies upon us without mentioning the Moon. As you know, the Moon circles the Earth every 28 days and we take the Moon with us on our annual journey around the Sun. The position of the Moon in relation to the Earth and the Sun has a tremendous effect on everything that lives on Earth. Of course, the Moon affects the tides. This has been brought home to me since we purchased a small boat and I have seen the high tides that are caused by the full and new Moon.

The Moon also affects women's menstrual cycles. I have also found that I get stronger responses to my meditations at the time of the full Moon. There are people who are adversely affected by the full Moon – it can make them feel 'hyper' and accentuates any mental disturbance they may suffer.

I must admit that although I knew all this I had never really understood why it should be so. In my research on the positive and negative ions in the atmosphere I found that the position of the Moon changes the number of positive ions in the atmosphere.

The Moon is positively charged – it is producing positive ions, so as it gets closer to the Earth it magnifies any stress and pollution that we are already sensing. As it gets closer it also increases the pressure of the Earth's atmosphere – it bears down on us, so to speak, and this is why the tides are accentuated.

The change in the content of the atmosphere as the

Moon comes nearer to us will take its toll on us too. We will generally be adversely affected by an increase in positive ions and the negative aspects of our life will be enhanced. We are affected on all levels, hence the emotional outbursts of some people and the mental instability of others.

What can we do about this? Well, we will definitely be affected the more we hold negative emotions and attitudes so there is only one thing we can do – lighten up. We must get more positive and work at letting go of the emotional baggage and negativity that we carry.

Exercise: Planetary Healing Meditation

Let's end this chapter with a simple distance healing exercise to help repair the damage humanity has done to the Earth. With this simple process we can help the birds, animals, rainforests, humankind – the entire environment of the planet and everything that lives on it.

- Inhale deeply four times. Relax your shoulders.
- Imagine that you are a great tree. Visualise and sense your roots growing deep into the Earth.
- Visualise a great beam of light pouring down from the sky, a laser of healing energy. Let this light fill every cell of your body and your entire aura with its strong healing vibrations.
- Pause for a moment while you become attuned to this divine energy.
- Imagine now that you are an astronaut high in the sky on a clear night. See the Moon and the stars and beneath you the planet Earth slowly rotating, lit by the light of the Moon.
- Draw the healing symbol in the air three times and direct

the healing energies from your hands towards the Earth.

- Think of sunny days, clear skies, rivers and streams of sparkling water, clear of all toxins and pollution.
- Think of mountains and lakes, see rainforests growing strong and untouched by humankind, filled with plants and flourishing wildlife.
- See wild animals free to roam without fear of human beings.
- Think of domestic and farm animals living in pleasant conditions with plenty of good food. See them respected and cared for by loving owners.
- See children playing, laughing and happy, well fed and well loved.
- See men and women caring for each other and their families. See neighbours and nations living in peace and harmony. See every person on Earth free from hunger and fear.
- See the entire planet spinning in a great ball of golden light.
- Imagine yourself stepping into the ball of light and feel yourself merging and becoming at one with the Earth. Spend a few moments in this state.
- Gradually come back into the room. Move your toes and fingers to help to bring you back.

In earlier chapters we looked at the way thoughts can affect us. We will now look at the worst scenario of negative thinking and how it can, either unintentionally or deliberately, become a curse. We shall see just how powerful curses can be and how these very darkest of negative thought forms can stay with families, passing down through generations and attaching themselves to objects and places for centuries.

7

Curses and Magic

In this chapter we will look at the way deliberate negative thoughts can create curses. We see the lasting and, in some cases, devastating effects of curses and how they can be cleared. What is the power of magic and what good and what harm can it do? We consider what it feels like to be under psychic attack and how we can protect ourselves.

The Power of Curses

Generally speaking, a curse is a deliberate invocation for misfortune to be brought down upon a person or group of people. Curses are wide-ranging in their power and effectiveness and many of them have been used for hundreds of years. A mild form would be a heat-of-the-moment outburst along the lines of: 'I hope your hair falls out.' A more serious attempt would call upon a series of calamities – or even a grisly death – to strike the victim. One's family and children may well be included in this profane and consciously venomous outpouring.

Fortunately not all curses will hit the mark. If the person invoking the curse doesn't really have evil intent in his heart (as in 'I hope your hair falls out') and is just using the opportunity to release anger, then the chances are that the victim will come off unscathed. And if the receiver is strong and fearless of the experience he or she will definitely not be affected.

If, however, the person uttering the curse means every word of their profanity and there is heartfelt emotion behind the words the effects can be disastrous, especially if the victim is frightened and weak in any way. In Africa it has been known for people to die just because they have been cursed or had a spell cast against them.

Although it's not unusual for people to swear and heavy language is quite normal in some sections of society, especially where a macho image is desired, cursing is not so prevalent as in the past. Once it was quite normal to curse someone who crossed your path, upset you in some way or caused you trouble. However, even casual cursing and swearing creates negative vibrations and is harmful to both those who say the words and those who hear and receive them.

If you find that you slip into swearing and cursing just take note that it is a negative activity. Remember that what you give out in vibrations will affect you directly, as the energy stream flows through your aura. You will also be affected by the law of cause and effect – 'what you reap you will sow'. If you are around people who curse readily then get into your egg and say to yourself with strong intention: 'Their negativity will have no effect on me whatsoever.'

The Power of Magic

When curses are combined with magic then we have serious problems. But what exactly is magic? Here is a simple list of definitions:

- Magic is using the power of the mind.
- Magic is the use of psychic and mystical abilities.
- Magic is the art of changing the form of energy – also called alchemy.

Magic is also a word we often give to any phenomenon we cannot understand that is beyond our current knowledge and comprehension. What is magical to people living in one age may seem quite normal and mundane to those living in another. For someone in the Middle Ages, the sight of a plane flying through the air would have been regarded as magical, as would most of our modern technology from the television to the telephone. A light coming from something other than a flame or the Sun would have been seen as a miracle.

We are creating new miracles in our own lifetime that will be normal in the future. For example, many people are now accessing the universal energy streams to help themselves and others to heal. By connecting to ancient symbols or by intentionally connecting to the universal energies of love we can invoke powerful healing forces. If the results seem miraculous, it is because until quite recently it was almost always doctors who cured people and doctors only use surgery and drugs as aids to healing.

Most doctors do not deliberately bring in powerful energies to help their patients to heal, and the medical profession has set the norms of health care and recuperation. This means that when people brought up with those norms see people being cured just by the intention of another person they may see it as magic – as a miracle. However, children who are being born now may well reach maturity thinking it is quite normal to visit a healer for certain ailments and diseases and won't be at all surprised by positive results.

The magical arts

The ancient arts of magic have always been shrouded in mystery so that ordinary people would not understand them. They were known to a privileged few and these enlightened ones made sure it stayed that way. Owing to their special knowledge and the secrecy surrounding their arts, the magicians of the past were powerful and respected.

If these 'magical' arts were taught at school then we would all see how they work and we could all perform them with ease. I can see a day coming when the secrecy will disappear as more and more people become aware of their personal power to use their mind and thought energy. I believe that everything is a form of energy – once we learn how to change energy forms we can all become magicians.

Once we learn the ability to see through and beyond the surface reality of things then we will have the basics for the greatest forms of magic. If we combine this change of perception with accepting our own power of mind and intention then we will truly live in the age of miracles – but then, what we now call miracles will just be normal everyday occurrences.

Witches – the healers of old

Before the days when Christianity came to Europe we had a different type of religion. We worshipped nature, as many cultures have done in the past. We saw the power of the Earth energies and acknowledged the sacred sites. We used these to connect with the energies and power of the Moon and the Sun and the other planets which affect our own. We acknowledged the spirits of the trees and mountains. We honoured them through ceremony and ritual, as did many ancient cultures in all parts of the world, from the Maoris of New Zealand and the Aboriginals of Australia to the Native Americans and the tribal peoples of South America and Africa.

Were we all wrong? Has every culture and people that has acknowledged the power of God through nature been stupid, wrong, even evil? I don't think so. However, for many centuries mainstream Christian Western societies have often seen these old ways as the ways of Satan – the work of the Devil – and have done their best to outlaw and destroy the old beliefs and thinking.

In former times every community had someone skilled in the arts of healing. These individuals learnt which plants could help and passed on the healing properties of trees, roots, flowers and so on to local people as tinctures, infusions and powders. These herbalist healers were usually older women who also acted as midwives and laid out the dead, so they played an important part in village life.

When Christianity came and we stopped worshipping nature, we still kept on our 'witches', as they were then called, because our new religion brought no alternatives to their healing ways. Although Christianity gave us a spiritual path to follow, the wisdom of the crones was not replaced.

White witches and black witches

As is often is the case, some witches turned their powers to negative ends and practised the dark arts, or 'black magic'. This is the practice of using the good powers of healing and distorting the energies to create disease, bad luck and curses. With their powers they could tap into the power of the universe and twist it to create a new form of energy – evil. Although just a few of the witches practised these dark arts, still the majority worked for the good of the villagers and the poor. However, they held positions of power in the villages, and the Church, which was run by men, decided to destroy the power of *all* the wise women of the villages.

Representatives of the Church began a systematic persecution through most of Europe. With this condemnation came a new attitude and the word 'witch' became associated with fear and evil. To differentiate between these two different types of witch we tend to call those who used their healing powers for good 'white witches' and those who used them for ill 'black witches'. There is a huge difference, but even now if I were to say the word witch to some of those I know in the Church I can feel them shudder!

Fortunately, the skills of the wise women were not entirely lost and the arts of the herbalist are widely practised again today. There are a number of specialist shops dispensing the old herbal remedies that can provide you with a herbal tincture or infusion for virtually any ailment or condition.

So the word 'witch' is much maligned. However, because we are looking at all the forms of negative energy that exist and seeing how we can combat it, protect ourselves against it and hopefully transform it, we must therefore first acknowledge that there are such evil arts practised in the world. There were people working with black magic in the past and there still are today.

Black Magic

As I said in the first chapter I learnt quite a lot about the effects of black magic when I lived in Malaysia and Africa. I can remember years ago a friend of mine dragging me reluctantly behind her as she searched through the suburbs of Johannesburg for a witchdoctor who was supposed to be able to help her get her boyfriend back. I felt extremely embarrassed about knocking on the side door of an enormous and very grand house and asking for the maid, who was a maid by day and a witchdoctor by night. Anyway, she gave my friend something to put into her bath and it worked!

Witchdoctors, shamans, medicine men, *bomo*s (Malaysia) and *sangoma*s (Africa) are some of the names given to people who practise the art of magic. They are predominantly working for the highest good of all and are mostly healers who do not practise black magic. However, there are some who do.

What is black magic?

Black magic is the deliberate distortion of good energy and the deliberate use of magic to bring detriment and harm to another. Mostly it is done for money. Someone will visit a black magician and pay them to bring someone else down – this could be a political opponent, an enemy, a neighbour who has upset them, a business rival or a member of the family who threatens to take something from them. In Africa it is rife.

If someone is doing well then they will be nervous that their friends, neighbours and other family members will go to a *sangoma* and organise a spell that will do them harm. If someone is doing exceptionally well they may be suspected of using a spell to bring them success, so their neighbours and fellow workers may think that it's only right to take their success away from them with magic too.

Types of black magic

Black magic comes in many forms. A simple spell can be created by mixing herbs and dried and ground-up animal parts. The witchdoctor will go into a trance by dancing, singing, chanting, ringing bells, gongs or cymbals, or by taking drugs. Then he or she will call out the curse or spell over the concoction to fill it with intention.

Another way they work is to take hair, nails or a photograph of the victim and use this as a 'target'. They then send malevolent thoughts to the target in a ritual connecting with a dark stream of energy invoked by a talisman or black magic object. In the same way that we may use a cross, a favourite crystal, a candle and so on to invoke the beautiful energies of love, so the dark practitioners will use objects to invoke their evil energies.

Practices at the very end of the dark spectrum will pervert recognised symbols of divinity and use them for their own ceremonies. For example, Hitler took the swastika and distorted what was a beautiful symbol used since ancient times by Buddhists and Hindus as a sign of purity. It is a truly powerful and loving symbol that adorns many temples and sacred places throughout Asia.

Hitler and his followers turned it into a symbol of evil and horror and it has taken some time for it to be cleared of its misuse. Satan-worshippers take the cross of Christianity and invert it. By such practices the energies of the power of good are diverted into a stream of darkness. But remember, if dark powers can take these things and change them, we can also claim them back again.

Clearing the effects of black magic

Light is stronger than darkness – we see this every time the Sun comes up, every time we light a candle, every time we turn on the light. Every time we do a good deed, every time we forgive someone who has harmed us and every time we give our love we turn around negativity. We transform dark to light. We can do the same to black magic and its results. Yes, it can do harm but it is possible to clear it and to heal the people affected. Here are just a few experiences that I have come across where the spell, curse or black magic has been cleared by bringing in the healing powers of light and love.

An experience in Singapore

A couple of years ago I visited Singapore to give workshops and healing sessions. In one workshop I had been talking about curses and their effects. In the tea-break a woman came up to me with a photograph and asked: 'Do you think you could take a look at my husband and see if you can help him?' As I took the photograph in my hand I felt the familiar feelings of dark energy – I felt a 'whoosh' of it going up my arm. I looked at the man in the photograph and sent healing to him and as I did I could feel a strong release and change come over me.

From this response I knew something powerful had happened. I handed back the photograph and said that I hoped I had been of some help to him. She thanked me and we continued with the workshop.

The next day the woman came up to me again. This time her face was covered in smiles and she said that she was to give me a big 'thank you' from her husband. She then explained what his problem had been and what had happened to him on that previous day. She told me that in the afternoon, just at the time of our tea-break, he had been at home using the vacuum cleaner when he suddenly felt a pain in his head.

He said it felt as though something was being pulled out of him. The pain was so strong that he had to sit down. He said that after a few moments, however, a great feeling of peace came over him. He felt as though something dreadful had been taken away from him.

Which in fact it had, and he knew it. A couple of years previously he had been a very successful businessman. He had been the top salesman of a team. Apparently there was a great deal of jealousy about his success and suddenly his whole life changed and he found he suddenly couldn't get any sales at all and his business totally collapsed. He lost his job and then to make bad matters worse he couldn't get a new job no matter what he tried. This is typical of a curse situation – no matter what you do you may find that you are thwarted.

The man went to several psychics and fortune-tellers, all of whom told him that he had been cursed. One of them told him that he would have to carry this curse for a while but eventually he would meet a European woman who would lift it for him! The last I heard he had started in a new job and all was going well.

A forceful clearing

A businessman came to one of my healing sessions and brought along his wife and two small children. For a year he had not been feeling his normal healthy, bright and energetic self. He had become tired and despondent and his work had been lacklustre; he felt he had lost his passion for life. He was an extremely spiritual man – a practising Buddhist – and he suspected that he was under the influence of some form of psychic attack. This is a broad description we use for any form of malevolence that is directed towards us from any source.

I had only just protected myself when I felt a great healing 'whoosh' come over me and then pass to this man. It was like a small whirlwind of light energy sweeping through us both and it swept away the influences of darkness. It happened so fast and with such force that his young son, who had been sitting on a chair next to me, was thrown off onto the floor. Fortunately he landed on his father's feet and no harm was done.

From that moment the man's zest for life returned and he has been going from strength to strength since then. Neither of us has discussed the source of his attack but I sensed it was probably a business-associated problem. I often get insights and often see symbols of what is the root cause of a problem, but if the situation is cleared up I don't search any further. I also don't want to encourage people to look for revenge or feel anything negative towards the perpetrators as this can just start the whole thing off again.

A curse from the past

A woman once came to me and asked me to check her past and see if I could see anything that might have caused an on-going problem in her family. 'Problem' is too light a word for it really – a series of tragedies would be nearer to the truth. In each of the last three generations one of the men in her family has been decapitated! Not something you expect in modern England but nevertheless, through accidents of one form or another, this gruesome fate had befallen three family members.

I connected with the woman and her family's energy stream and I saw a very black and tropical scene of voodoo-style black magic. I told her what I was picking up and I asked her if anyone in her family had had anything to do with this in the past. She remembered that her great-grandfather or great-great-grandfather had been a missionary in Haiti but his work had not been well accepted there and he and his family had left quickly.

Haiti is renowned for its powerful brand of magic associated with the traditional religion called voodoo, a mix of West African nature worship with Roman Catholic elements. Christian missionaries in the past tried to suppress voodoo as an evil pagan cult, and perhaps this led to my client's ancestor being cursed by a voodoo magician. Anyway, we cleared the curse. So far, the rest of her family have been safe.

How hate can harm

We can produce the effects of black magic without going to a witchdoctor or casting spells. A concoction of hate and fear empowered with the intention to do harm is enough to produce a dark stream of energy that will make a healthy person sick, affecting their mind and their physical state.

I came across an example of this quite recently. I had a call from a friend of mine who was in trouble. Let me call her Lucy. Her boyfriend was from the Middle East and they had started to live together in a city in south-east Asia. The boyfriend – we shall call him Jamed – had a big problem. His mother had been ringing continually to harass him for some time. The reason? He was officially engaged to another woman in his own country. This was an arranged engagement and the marriage was supposed to take place in three months.

Jamed had no desire or intention to marry his arranged bride. He loved his mother but he had been away from home some time and was looking to make his future in Asia. The family were distraught, as the rejection of the bride would bring shame to the family name. Jamed explained to his mother that he was in love with another woman, Lucy, and he asked her to free his fiancée to find another husband who could fulfil all his marital obligations.

For a while all went quiet, then Lucy started to feel really ill. She had the most dreadful headaches and started to be overcome by feelings of panic and fear. Jamed was away travelling with his work so she called in two friends of mine, one of whom is a well-known local healer. They went to her house and as they got to the garden gate both women started to get dreadful pains in their heads.

By the time my healer friend had crossed half the garden she was violently sick. They quickly protected themselves and continued into the house. Lucy was in a bad way and was also vomiting and suffering extremely bad headaches. They immediately suspected that someone had put some spell or curse on Lucy and called me on the phone.

I connected with Lucy and then followed an energy trail back to Jamed's mother and his estranged fiancée. I felt a stream of dark and turgid energy flowing between them and Lucy. I cleared the energy and connected to Jamed's mother to try to explain to her on a spiritual level that this was no way to solve the problem. I picked up a great stream of hate and fear.

I saw that Jamed's mother, a Muslim, had felt the antagonism that many in the West had directed towards Muslims after the 11 September attack in New York. She had related to the apprehension and fear felt by many of her faith at that time, many of whom were filled with dread that America and other Western countries would start a full-scale war against Islam.

In her mind she saw her son as having been 'captured' by 'the enemy', and she had also linked into the stream of hate energy that the al-Qa'eda terrorists were projecting towards the West at that time. This was enough to surround Lucy and her home with dark vibrations. In this instance I don't think deliberate black magic was used but the effects of the energies of hate and fear had the same result.

After I had cleared the spell, all the women recovered and my friends spent some time clearing the house of all residual negativity by smudging and spraying with flower and crystal essences.

Protect yourself

There may be times in your own life when you experience the jealousy or anger of someone. You may feel their antagonism. You may not have such a strong reaction as Lucy but you may find that you feel uncomfortable, emotional or drained of energy. If you suspect or fear that someone is sending you bad thoughts and vibrations then you need to protect yourself. At the end of this chapter I have described several ways in which you can guard yourself from any form of negative thought stream, whether it be jealousy or, in extremely rare instances, a curse.

On the other hand, if you are feeling a little guilty that your own thoughts towards another person have been negative, just stop speaking and thinking badly of them and intend to send them a beam of light. Whenever you start to think negative thoughts redirect your mind either to ignore the thoughts entirely or to send the person light. Even if they have upset you, the last thing that you want to do is get into the habit of sending out negative vibrations – this will be harmful for both of you. It won't change the other person for the better and it will be detrimental to you as well.

Modern Magic

We have recently seen a spate of books and films about magic, the best known being *Harry Potter* and *The Lord of the Rings*. These have brought the subject of magic, spells, curses and alchemy into the public arena. I personally love these books and all well-crafted fantasy novels as I think they help us open our minds to the unbelievable. This will eventually assist us in accepting the amazing events which we will see in the future.

We are moving towards a time when more and more people will develop psychic powers and these powers are going to be ever more readily accepted. Eventually there will come a time when they will be commonplace and used by all in their daily lives. Everyone will be able to learn to perform amazing acts – what we call miracles – just as so many people are now able to perform natural energy healing thanks to the introduction of Reiki.

Over the next couple of generations we will see extraordinary changes – not so much through technology, although that is leading us there, but through the power of our own minds. Once people know and accept the great power of their minds and thoughts and realise that they can create and draw into their lives what they need, then we will move into incredible times.

However, we need to learn how to use these new powers productively and harmlessly. Just as we are now learning to understand the potential dangers as well as the benefits of our modern technologies, and learning how we can neutralise these hazards, we also need to be aware that the power of the mind can be used negatively – as we have seen in this chapter.

The interest in magic that *Harry Potter* and other books and films have brought with them has spawned a crop of books about magic, which have mostly been aimed at teenage and younger readers. I recently bought one of the teenage magazines and in it there are a number of spells including, and I quote, 'To snag a boyfriend', 'To have a perfect date', and so on.

The examples were innocuous enough and books that show young girls how to gain power over boys and how to get them to fall in love also seem like harmless fun. However, if you work with spells it is essential that you remember that there is *power* in your words and *power* in your intentions. If by any means you do harm to another then this is bound to come back to you through natural law.

If you don't act for the highest good, with the very best intentions for everyone involved, then your negative act will come back to you at least tenfold. In other words what you give out you will get back. This is a natural law of the universe, a law of life. You will get back love if you give out love, but if you give out bad vibes or wish harm upon others then eventually harm will come back to you. So be careful with spells – no matter how simple they seem, they will have power and they will have repercussions.

By the way, if you do want to get a new partner then use a positive declaration to the universe that you want the best boyfriend or girlfriend possible. Say it out loud and then visualise yourself happy with a kind and attractive partner. We have seen how to create and attract what you need in the section called 'Creating Positive Situations' in Chapter 2 and the accompanying exercise 'Bring positive things into your life' (see page 63).

Dealing with Psychic Attacks

Curses, spells and any form of black magic and malevolent thoughts are all forms of psychic attack. How do you know if you are under attack and what can you do if you are affected? Here are some of the symptoms of a psychic attack:

- Nightmares.
- Feeling your hair standing on end, either on your neck or arms.
- 'Cobwebby' feelings indicating the presence of negative energy.
- Sudden bouts of fear for unknown reasons, accompanied by pounding heart and sweating.
- Clamminess and perspiration.
- A sensation of being under physical attack.
- Nausea and sickness.
- Severe headache.

- A sense of loss of control – suddenly feeling emotionally unstable.

Night attack

I will try to explain what psychic attack feels like as I have been attacked on several occasions for one reason or another. Once when I was working overseas I woke up in the night and my heart was thudding. I felt sure that someone was in the room but when I put on the light there was no one there although I could still feel the terror racing through me. I realised that I was probably being psychically attacked so I went into counter-attack.

First I needed to protect myself, so I envisaged myself being surrounded by light. If you cannot visualise well you can just say 'I am surrounded by light' – this is definitely easier if you are a little scared. I then told myself that there was nothing to fear – which of course there wasn't as no one was actually in the room. I called in my angels and spiritual guides to help me. I then sent out waves and waves of light.

I then realised that whoever it was must be quite scared of me, otherwise why would they bother to attack me? My intentions throughout that trip were to help others so it would seem that whoever was attacking me was trying to stop me doing something good. This was a major insight that has helped me ever since. If I were weak and harmless they surely wouldn't be bothering with me, so they must be afraid of my strength. That was a reassuring thought!

Gradually my heart stopped thumping and I felt OK. I lit a candle and sprayed the room and after a while all the negativity cleared away. I don't know who or what had attacked me but I had planned the next day to carry out a major clearing of spirits from a school and I suspected it was something to do with this. The next day my husband rang me and told me he had had nightmares that night and had woken up feeling a threat. He had just told it to 'b— off' and kept the light on for the rest of the night and gone back to sleep – which is another way of handling it!

Every time either my husband or myself has been threatened the other one has felt it too. Sometimes I have felt that the attack has actually been directed at him and I notice that it normally happens when we are apart, when our energies cannot be combined so easily.

Longer-term effects of psychic attack

The effects of a curse over a longer period can be many and varied, but these are some of the signs:

- A feeling that you are cursed.
- Marked loss of confidence.
- Complete lethargy and lack of energy that came upon you suddenly.
- Bad luck – nothing goes your way, no matter what you do.
- All your ventures are thwarted even when you keep a positive attitude.
- A series of unexplained accidents and health problems.
- A recurring feeling of being threatened for no apparent reason.
- Sudden mood swings and emotional outbursts for no apparent reason.

Most people who come to me for a clearing know within themselves when they have been cursed and they usually know why and when it happened. It's not a condition that's going to strike someone out of the blue for no reason. However, you may be affected by the jealousy or dislike of someone who can be thinking badly of you without you knowing it. The outcome of this can be similar, although not as powerful as a full-blown spell or curse.

Ways to protect yourself from psychic attack

I have already introduced you to a number of ways to protect yourself against negativity but here are some particularly powerful protections that you can use against a psychic attack. To be fearless is the greatest protection of all, because dark energies are attracted to the lower vibrations of our fear. If you can put yourself into a state of total calm and fearlessness you will have little trouble with these negative energies. This may seem difficult, but you may find that the following methods help you to let go of your fear.

The protection symbol

The symbol of the Pyramid and Eye of Horus (see the following page) is a powerful protective amulet against curses and other forms of psychic attack. Draw the symbol in the air three times in front of you, or over someone you wish to protect. Start at the middle of the bottom line of the pyramid and draw the outline with two hands, meeting at the top. Draw the eye from left to right clockwise then draw the iris as a dot last of all.

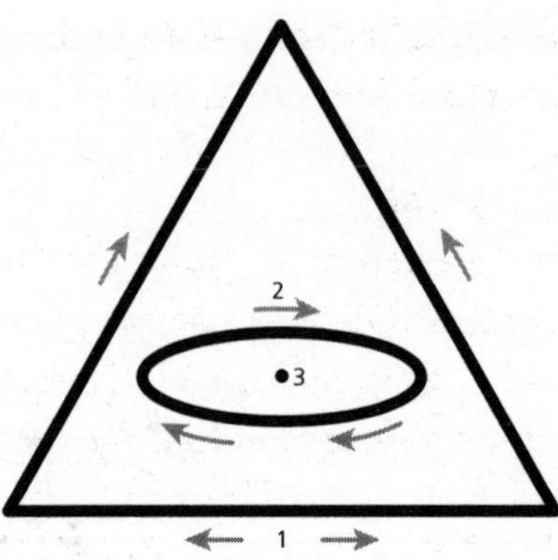

The protection symbol combines the Pyramid and the Eye of Horus, two powerful ancient Egyptian symbols.

The four trees

I was taught this powerful visualisation technique by a woman in Hong Kong. It has worked very well for me and other people who have used it. Imagine that you are surrounded by four huge trees, and that wrapped around the trees from top to bottom are golden chains – gold has particular protective properties. Visualise a beam of white light coming down upon you and immersing you in its wonderful presence. Know you are totally protected.

Golden pyramid

This visualisation is explained more fully in Chapter 3. Imagine yourself or the person you are protecting surrounded by a golden pyramid and see the pyramid filled with golden light.

Running water

I have read that a powerful attack cannot touch you if you are standing under running water. This is probably a good idea if you find that your mind seems to be taken over and you can't think straight. Get under the shower to get your head straight then use the other visualisations and protections that I have mentioned here.

Amulets and crystals

In Chapter 3 we looked at crystals that have particular protective properties. Of these aegirine has particularly strong protective powers against black magic and curses. Most religions have potent spiritual symbols that you can draw in the air or wear as amulets to ward off any negative energy attack. For example, the Christian cross is extremely effective as a form of protection. It isn't necessary for you to be religious to use one of these symbols, but it is important to have faith and trust in their power.

Blessings

You can get a protective blessing from any spiritual leader or teacher. Some Buddhist monks will bless you and then tie a thread around your wrist that will stay with you for a long time and 'hold' their blessing in place.

Spirit guides and angels

We all have helpers in the spirit world who look over us, protect us and guide us through life. Call upon them to protect you or your loved ones especially when you feel there is danger. Angels will come to your aid if you call them and sometimes they will appear in human form to help us. The Archangel Michael has an army of angels who will fight evil and darkness and he will come whenever called to surround you with protective light and take away your fear.

EXERCISE: A RITUAL TO CLEAR A CURSE OR SPELL

A curse is created with intention so we use intention to dissolve it. It is created with evil intention so we clear it with love and good intention. As most serious curses and spells are cast using ritual and symbols, we use the same methods to dispel them. Only perform the following ritual if you feel confident and happy about it – don't do it with fear as it will make it difficult for you to be in the state of peace and love that is necessary for the ritual to be effective. The person you perform this for can be present in person or you can use a photograph. You can also perform the ritual for yourself.

- Find a quiet and peaceful location with good vibrations. If you have a sacred place to use so much the better.
- Place a small bowl of water containing sea or rock salt in the room. This will collect the negativity you release – make sure you throw this away somewhere safe afterwards, like down a drain.
- If you are helping someone else and they are with you, get them to sit or lie down and make them comfortable and cosy by covering them with a rug or towel.
- Protect yourself by visualising the purple flame around you, protecting you from all negativity.
- Call down the Archangel Michael, the angel who fights evil. He is also the great angelic protector. You can also call down any spiritual leader with whom you associate, such as Jesus or the Buddha.
- Light a candle and visualise its light filling the room, representing divine light.
- If you have any favourite crystals or pictures of spiritual teachers place them around the candle – this will show your affinity to the healing powers of nature and to those unseen helpers in the spirit world that look over us and help us in these situations.
- Stand in front of the person you are clearing, or their photograph.

- Draw the release symbol three times and then the healing symbol three times to raise the energies. Allow yourself to be a channel for the very highest spiritual and divine energies to flow through you.
- Placing your hand on the person's head, or on their photograph, say: 'I clear all curses and spells affecting you – NOW.' If you want to be absolutely confident say this three times. You and the person you are helping will feel the energy change once the spell or curse is dissolved.
- Draw the protection symbol (see page 240) over the other person.
- Sweep your hands through their aura for a few moments then continue to fill them with loving energy until they feel peaceful. They may feel slightly disorientated or 'spaced out' afterwards so don't let them drive for a while.
- Finally, draw the stabilising symbol (below) in the air to stabilise the cleared energies. Draw the top cup followed by the bottom cup and then the line down the middle.

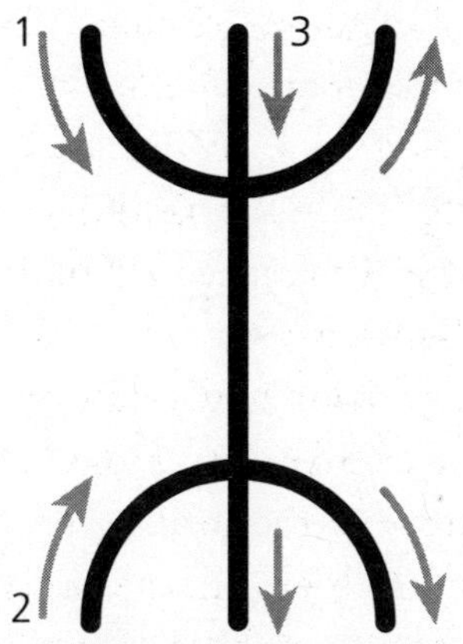

The stabilising symbol is used to fix the cleared energies after dissolving a curse or spell.

Remember that the incidence of curses is small. After reading this chapter please don't start to imagine that every headache is a sign that you have been cursed! Keep yourself physically and spiritually strong and keep affirming the positive in your life and you are unlikely to be affected.

In the next chapter we are going to look at another subject that can be a source of a great deal of anxiety – spirits and ghosts. However, as we shall see, many of our fears about the presence of spirits and souls that have yet to leave the Earth are unnecessary, and there are numerous ways in which we can help them to move on.

8

Spirit Presence

We will now look at why some souls do not move on to the astral planes of the spirit world but stay around the places they inhabited when they were alive. I will go into some of the problems that their presence may cause us and how we can help them to move on to their final destination. We also look at those evolved beings from the spirit world who bring us love and beautiful experiences.

The Experience of Death

In normal circumstances the experience of death is a beautiful one as the soul returns home. It is completely natural and it can be a loving and peaceful experience for the departing soul. Of course, there may be suffering and trauma in the time leading up to death, but as we pass over peace and love surround us and our pain and suffering cease.

The soul leaves the physical body and moves through what seems like a tunnel as it goes from the denseness of the physical world to the world of spirit. Here a welcome party of relations and friends meets the soul – for this is, after all, a homecoming. Our lives on Earth are journeys away from home, journeys of discovery and growth. We come to Earth to discover more about ourselves and to learn how to be loving beings, through all the challenges, tests and trials that life down here brings.

The progress to enlightenment

Once we have arrived on the other side we go through a period of self-evaluation with the help of our spirit guides (our helpers in the spirit world) to see how we have managed on this last Earth trip and how we have coped with the challenges that we faced there. Following this assessment we can acknowledge our weaknesses and determine the work that we still need to do in order to progress our evolution towards the state of bliss and enlightenment which is the destination of all souls.

Our soul continues with this work, helped all the time by our guides and spiritual advisers, until we reach a point where we all decide that the soul is ready for its next incarnation. For an excellent account of and clear insight into our existence between lives I recommend *Journey of Souls* and *Destiny of Souls* by Michael Newton (see Further Reading, page 283). He is a hypnotherapist specialising in past-life regression who through hypnotherapy has taken hundreds of patients back through their lives and specifically to the 'interlife', the time between lives. Through his examination of their experiences he has documented many interesting facts of the interlife and the world of spirit.

Brian Weiss is another hypnotherapist who has written extremely clear accounts of past-life regression, recording the previous lives and interlife experiences of his patients. I can also recommend his book, *Many Lives, Many Masters* (see Further Reading).

Is there a hell?

This is one of the most frequently asked questions on the subject of life after death. I personally don't think so. Whenever I take myself or others back to the place we visit between lives we always see a place of great beauty. However, I think we make this place whatever we like. In other words, we create the images that make us feel at home and make what we feel we need and what we deserve. Of course we don't really need images of forms in the interlife as we are spiritual beings and therefore have no physical form. However, we feel more at ease and can relate far more easily to our new surroundings if we see familiar shapes, scenery and beings. So, although it is not necessary, initially we will see people as we knew them and we will see scenery that is familiar to us. As we become adjusted to being back home in the spirit world so the need for form may become less.

I have regressed to two of my interlife periods and saw two very different scenes. In the first life I was a Chinese woman and when I died and passed over I saw a very similar scene to the one that had surrounded my earthly home in southern China. In the second life I was an English missionary and had spent much of my time in Africa. However, as I loved my homeland passionately my return 'home' to the spirit world took me to rolling hills typical of pastoral England.

So if heaven is what we make it, hell is too. If we die

fearful of the consequences of our life, with expectations of going to a dark and gruesome place then that is where we will go. If we think we deserve to suffer for any dark deeds we have perpetrated on Earth then we will go to our own form of hell.

When I have contacted spirits I have sometimes seen them walking around with their heads down, unable to see the divine light above them that beckons them to higher vibrations and planes of existence. They seem to be totally despondent and suffering all sorts of mental torment in a very dark and gloomy place. Fortunately, they often only stay there for a short time and soon realise that they can move on (although time is an earthly notion and means little to those on the other side).

The main reason why many souls have created hell for themselves is that many preachers and spiritual leaders in the past taught that we would go to hell if we sinned. So it is just such a place that a soul will imagine for itself if it feels guilty for its deeds on Earth. The fear of this can also make some souls hang around on the earthly plane for some time after death.

One question that often arises when we talk about death is: 'How can we meet a member of our family who has died before us, if they have reincarnated?' When you are born you only send down a certain amount of your essence – your soul – and some part of you stays behind in the heavenly realms so you are able to meet loved ones when they die and pass over.

Ghosts

Now let's look at the reasons why some souls don't pass straight over to the other side. How would you know if your home has a spirit presence? What do these spirits – or ghosts – feel like and look like? I have explained several times the clues that alert you to the presence of negative energy such as cold areas, 'cobwebby' and clammy feelings, your hair standing on end. If you have a spirit in the house you will experience these symptoms with a vastly increased intensity. To me the feelings are much stronger and more localised and quite obvious once I have opened to them.

Sometimes you will sense a spirit's energy whether you open up or not, especially when the spirit wants to make contact. You may also see an apparition, which is a denser form of spirit energy – so dense, in fact, that you can see it, albeit in a rather ethereal form.

You may also be able to see spirits with your inner sight – they will appear like video clips being played inside your head. This is how I see them and communicate with them. They will show themselves to you as they think best, but normally it will be in the same state as when they died. This makes it easier for you to understand something about them – their sex, age and the era in which they died, which you can see from their mode of dress.

Why some souls stay earthbound

There are several reasons why a soul will stay on the Earth and haunt the locality of its last existence.

Sudden death

Occasionally someone will die suddenly and the transition from life to death is so unexpected that the soul may not grasp that it has, in fact, died. The cause of death is often a fatal accident like a car or plane crash. These unfortunate souls may then wander around the accident location for a while in a disoriented state. Fortunately, this situation is generally only temporary. Such spirits are commonly found at the sides of motorways due to the number of fatal accidents and pile-ups that occur on them. It is easy to help such souls to move on and we shall see how to do this a little later.

A desire to take care of those left behind

This again is often a temporary situation although it may last for some time. If a person who dies has a particularly strong attachment to someone living they sometimes stay around with the intention of helping their bereaved loved one. This most often happens when the survivor was dependent on the one who died.

These souls stay with the best of intentions and with gentle persuasion they move on easily enough. They don't intentionally cause any problems – in fact some people who can sense them may get some comfort from their presence. However, their spirit's presence may 'spook' the person who is left behind and trying to carry on with his or her life.

(It is in fact quite normal for a soul to stay around for a short while after death before it travels on. You may have had experience of this yourself and many people see or feel the presence of a family member or friend who has died in the few days immediately following their death. They will often give you a sign of their presence that is unmistakably associated with them – for example, I knew when my father-in-law was around us shortly after his death by the smell of his pipe. Such short visits are a way to show you that they are just fine, that life does continue – and that there is life after death.)

Sadness at leaving

Some people are very attached to their homes and possessions. This can be another reason that can delay the departure of a soul. I once was asked to help the spirit of an old lady who was present in my friend's cottage. Several times I attempted to get her to move on but she was quite obstinate and when I asked her why she wouldn't go she told me in no uncertain terms: 'This is my home and I like it here.' What can you say to that?

Apart from making the part of the house that she favoured a little cold, her presence was no problem so she and my friend continued to share the house quite amicably!

Anger and revenge

Souls that are bitter are the angry ghosts that people often refer to as 'evil spirits'. I personally don't buy into the theory of evil spirits. The word 'evil' is an evocative word that is associated with fear so I try to avoid it where possible. After all, every spirit is just another soul like us trying to get along in the world, trying to work out how to become more evolved, and some of them manage it a little better than others. Most anger is caused by previous hurt and I try to bear that in mind when helping these souls to move on. They can be more difficult to deal with and may try to scare us as their anger will feed on our fear. Very often they are the victims of murder and violent death and they hold on to the emotion that they were experiencing when they died.

There are many books about such ghosts haunting old buildings – with or without their heads! Their negative energy causes the atmosphere to drop in temperature dramatically. They can make noises – like the chains I heard in my childhood home. They can create smells and even sights to show their displeasure. Personally I haven't come across too many of these. Most of the spirits I connect with are sad and lost rather than angry and abusive. If in doubt leave these spirits for an expert to clear.

Guilt and fear

As we have seen, a soul may be so frightened of going to hell that it stays close to Earth rather than take the risk of moving on. It needs to be persuaded that it will not end up in a dark region of dire punishments or fire.

These earthbound spirits tend to be drawn to places with geopathic stress where the atmosphere is rarer and therefore it is easier for them to exist – the denser and lower-vibration energies are closer to their own. It would seem that negative energies created by the Earth act as a magnet for any lost or wandering soul that is in a distressed or angry state. This is the reason why it is sometimes possible to clear a location of its visitor only to find that a short while later another has taken its place.

Poltergeists and mischievous spirits

Poltergeists are very disturbed spirits that can use incredible energy to move things around in homes. Some people say that poltergeist activity is caused by energy created unconsciously by youngsters and teenagers when they are going through their difficult and disturbed years of growing up.

Well, young people may on occasions cause chaotic energies and from my experience that is very likely. However, spirits can make things move, especially when they want to attract attention to their plight.

I had a call one day from a friend who asked me to go and help her with a disturbance in her home. On three consecutive days the mirror above her dressing table had been thrown onto the floor. I say 'thrown' but 'placed' is probably a better word as it wasn't damaged on any of these occasions, nor was anything on the dressing table affected. It was a heavy mirror and its setting and fixings were firm and still in place. My friend guessed that this was the work of a disturbed spirit as she could sense its presence.

I opened myself to the energies of the spirit and made connection with a lady who was absolutely desolate. She was sobbing and asked if I could help her to leave now and move on. She went easily – she just needed a little help to raise her energies enough to help her move into the light. She was truly desperate and had obviously tried to get the attention of my friend by resorting to the drastic measure of moving her mirror.

I have never personally experienced a full-blown poltergeist situation, although a friend of mine had her wardrobe thrown over in her haunted house. Poltergeists can be quite destructive and there is no doubt about their presence when they are in full swing. Furniture can be thrown around and articles will be seen to move through the air without any reason.

The nearest I came to such an experience in my own home was at a time when I was leaving my house in Hertfordshire in England and moving to South Africa to live. I had a weekend house party to say farewell to my closest friends.

I hadn't been aware of a presence in that house but on this particular weekend we had three unexpected and unaccountable incidents which made me think that the house spirit wasn't too keen on my departure.

First, a plant pot fell off a table right behind where my mother and one of my friends were sitting chatting. I accused my mother of knocking it with her chair but they both swore they hadn't touched it and in fact they were sitting about a foot in front of it. Then, in the kitchen, a china teapot flew off the work surface and broke on the floor. There had been no one in the kitchen at the time and the pot had been placed far back on the surface.

The third event happened in the garden. I had separated out the plates that I was planning to leave for the incoming tenants and the rest I put outside on the patio table. I came inside to chat with my friends and about ten minutes later the plates suddenly flew off the table onto the ground. I definitely had a strong feeling that this was a message from the house spirit to tell me that it didn't approve of my leaving!

Child spirits

Child spirits in a house can be mischievous. A young girl spirit lived with us in our house in Kuala Lumpur. She seemed to enjoy playing tricks on us and was constantly hiding small things – it was she who hid my ring, as I recounted in Chapter 6. The items usually turned up, sometimes on the same day or a day later, and very often not far from where they had been. Sometimes she returned them to their original position. She took a delight in hiding my husband's credit cards, for example, and many times I would put a pen down and then turn around and find it had disappeared. Her best trick – although it wasn't so funny for us – was her paint hoax.

We had been back to England on holiday and while we were away my housekeeper Saro had taken the opportunity to spring clean the house, including cleaning all our clothes and tidying them away and washing all the curtains. We came back and after the usual amazing welcome from our two dogs I started to climb the stairs to the bedroom. I couldn't believe what I saw – the long white net curtains on the stairwell windows were covered in a brown substance. It looked as if someone had flicked and smeared paint all over them.

I called Saro and asked her what had happened. She screamed. 'They went up clean yesterday,' she cried. We then found that various outfits in my wardrobe and some of Tony's shirts were also covered in this substance. It all washed out without any trouble but for weeks we would find clothes that were perfectly clean one day but had these marks on them the next. When I told one of my friends she said that it was a form of 'psychic paint'. Just like invisible ink the colour doesn't show for a while but then as time goes by it gradually appears.

This episode occurred just after we had found out that we would be moving to Hong Kong – so I guess it was our spirit's way of showing her disapproval of our departure. She also played a little trick on the next people who moved into the house. One day they came into their lounge to find that all the figurines in the display cabinet had been turned around to face the wall. I expect they had also upset her in some way, although they blamed the maid as they didn't believe in ghosts.

Another of her favourite tricks, which she performed quite often, was to rumple up the covers in the downstairs bedroom, usually after the maid had tidied and cleaned it and before a visitor arrived – maybe she was trying to get the maid into trouble! I tried to persuade the spirit to leave on many occasions but she wasn't interested – I think she was having too much fun tormenting the household.

Portals and corridors

Another quite disturbing but interesting phenomenon is the existence of a portal in your home. Portals are spots of rarefied atmosphere, like small sacred sites. They are not negative and they are specifically for spirits to move into the other realms – spiritual gateways to the astral planes.

I can speak from experience here as I have had a portal in each of my last three homes. I suspect it is the same one that comes with me when I move to a new house.

Because of the portal in my home I have a constant stream of etheric beings moving through the house, which is why so many of my visitors are convinced that our house is haunted. I have always denied this and for some of my friends reading this book this will be the first time they have heard about our spiritual gateway. It is in our upstairs guest room and, of course, located directly on the ley line that runs through the house. I feel fine about it and am happy to live with it.

Another explanation for a stream of spirit visitors can be that your home acts as an 'etheric corridor'. In Kuala Lumpur one of my friends lived in an apartment block located between a Chinese temple and cemetery. Needless to say she was always feeling the presence of the stream of migrants moving from one to the other and for some reason they favoured her apartment, maybe because she was sympathetic to them and acknowledged their presence without fear. Sometimes they could be a bit annoying – especially when they woke up her son, who would complain about the man in the room!

Beware of the Ouija

While I am talking about the spirit world and its effects

on us I would like to tell you a little story by way of a warning. This is about an experience involving Michael, the man who had such a draining influence on my energy through my wedding ring in Chapter 4.

This happened one weekend in the winter when I was in my mid-twenties. I was visiting an old friend in Essex and we had been discussing my life and where I was going. My first husband and I were separated, I was a single woman again and I knew that I had reached a crossroads in my life. It had been a pretty emotional time for me and I was looking for guidance. I had applied for a couple of new jobs and sought help in deciding which way I should go.

It had crossed my mind to go to a local fortune-teller but she was completely booked up for that particular weekend so my friend and I decided we would try to ask the spirit world directly for help. My grandmother came into my mind and I suggested we try to connect to her.

My friend said that she had heard that lighting a candle would help me to get through, so we turned down the lights and lit a candle. I closed my eyes and, holding my topaz drop, thought of my grandmother. Almost immediately I saw her in my mind's eye. I was very excited, but then she told me emphatically to stop this communication and go to an experienced medium if I wanted to make contact. So I stopped.

The next day my friend's boyfriend and Michael joined us and we told them what had happened. Michael immediately suggested we try using the Ouija, which is a way of connecting to the spirit world. He explained how it works. You take twenty-six small pieces of paper on which you write the letters of the alphabet. You lay these out in a circle and then place a glass in the middle. The members of the group each place a finger on the glass and ask questions. The glass then moves to the letters and spells out the answers.

I thought this sounded like a good idea and Michael had just the place for us to do this. He had a friend with a house set in the middle of its own land a few miles away from where we were. It was getting dark by the time we arrived at what seemed a really desolate spot – there were acres of land and the house was truly far from anywhere. There was no one at home when we arrived but Michael knew where the key was kept and let us in. I was beginning to have doubts at this stage – the place was large and without its owners seemed cold and unfriendly. However, they had a large lively black dog that did its best to welcome us.

We went into the dining room, which was a dark, panelled room with trophies and guns on the wall – it seemed the owner was a keen sportsman (which should have been enough to get me out of the place straight away). We set up the Ouija letters and glass and started asking questions. We immediately had a response and we started to find the whole event quite exciting and exhilarating.

I asked about my job and received the answer I wanted. I also asked a health question for my mother and again got a good answer. We each took turns to sit outside the circle and write down the answers to prove that no one was deliberately moving the glass, but the glass seemed to have a life of its own and shot around the circle with us hardly touching it.

Then things changed. Michael said that he wanted to ask a question but he didn't want to tell us what it was. He said he would do it in his head. It was my turn to sit outside the circle. I was trying to understand the replies he was getting when I realised that they were in

Italian, Michael's native language. Then I spelt out three or four short repeated words, which we later realised translated as 'go, go, go'. The glass stopped and we all looked at Michael, who was looking white and quite strange.

Suddenly I felt a chill and I started to shiver. Then my friend jumped up and cried: 'Oh, I am so cold!' and became quite agitated. Her boyfriend also jumped up with the same reaction. Then it reached me. I was completely overwhelmed by a great coldness and felt as though I were losing control. I cried out and my two friends, bless them, realised what was happening and pulled me out of the room and together we recited the Lord's Prayer.

Gradually the feeling left me. I felt myself coming back and I could hear the dog barking as it ran round and round the house and I noticed that the hair on its back was standing up. It was obviously very frightened and spooked. It wasn't the only one.

We left the house immediately and I asked Michael what had he been doing. He said that he had made contact with his mother and he had asked her to get a spirit to put a curse on his ex-girlfriend. Of course, this is the worst thing he could possibly have done and we were all affected by the negative energies that he had invoked with this horrible request. His mother had seen this trouble coming and had called for us to leave.

That was my first and last experience of the Ouija. I strongly advise you never, never to use it as you have no control over who or what may come through to you. My grandmother's advice was good – if you want to connect to your dead relatives or friends then go to an experienced medium. Naturally this was the last time I saw Michael. Fortunately, since my twenties when this incident took place, my discernment has improved and I have better judgement of the character of the people with whom I associate.

Releasing Souls to the Light with Love

We'll now look at how we can release souls and help them to move on. This is fulfilling and beautiful work and is greatly beneficial not only to you and the environment but also a wonderful service to the soul that is having difficulties leaving the Earth plane. Of course each situation is different. However, there are certain basic steps to follow that will work most of the time.

I should point out here that as with all healing you are only offering a helping hand. You may well find that your offer of help is rejected if the soul has a strong desire to stay put, like the old woman in my friend's cottage and the young girl in my home in Kuala Lumpur, who were not at all interested in moving on.

I asked a number of my other psychic friends to try to get the girl to go but they all received the same 'No, thank you' response – much to the annoyance of the maid! Free will still rules in the spirit world.

When a spirit is causing havoc and is even harmful you can ask evolved spirits from the other side to help and they have authority to be more forceful. For example, the Archangel Michael leads a host of warrior angels who can be extremely strong and powerfully persuasive when necessary.

I will now explain the process I use to assist spirits to move on – of course, you can modify this to suit yourself and the circumstances. I will follow this with three instances where these and similar techniques have been used successfully.

Exercise: Helping Souls to the Light

I suggest that you do this work away from the actual location. It is just as effective as being there in person and it will be less challenging for you. For this exercise you will need a plan or photograph of the place inhabited by the spirit and your dowsing pendulum.

- Find a quiet and peaceful place.
- Protect yourself by visualising yourself immersed in a violet flame.
- Call upon your guides and angels to be with you. Call upon Archangel Michael to be with you.
- Breathe deeply. Open yourself with the intention of sensing the spirits in your chosen location.
- Use your pendulum to find out:
  - * Are there any spirits present?
  - * If so, how many are there?
  - * Any other facts you want to know (for example, the sex and age of the spirit and when it died).
- Close your eyes and place your hands on the plan of the place you are clearing. Connect to the spirits and one by one ask them to leave. Don't worry if you cannot 'see' the spirits – if you sense their presence that is good enough. Here are a few things you can say to them:
- Ask them if they want help. If you don't get an answer proceed anyway. They will only go if they wish.
- Tell them that you wish them no harm and are there to help them.
- Tell them that they have died and it is time for them to move on.
- Tell them that they are going back to somewhere beautiful where they will be welcomed by their loved ones.
- Tell them there is nothing to fear – they are not going to hell.

- Call the angels and tell the spirit to look up to the light. You will see the light in your mind's eye – this is the light that signifies the higher realms of the astral planes (or heaven or the interlife – or whatever you wish to call it).
- Imagine that you are helping the spirit and caring for it. See it go up to join the light. Send lots of love with it. In your mind's eye you may see cherubs come down to help the spirit, especially if it is a child, or you may see angels or Jesus or other spiritual figures coming to help them. But even if you see nothing, just trust in the process.

Releasing a group of spirits

A large group of spirits was trapped in the basement of the house where I lived in Malaysia. They were having a very bad effect on the energies of the room, which was a guest room, and also on the lounge directly above it. I was having problems with the dogs who were generally well behaved and house-trained but every now and again (on the full Moon!) would mess in the lounge above the guest room. And they absolutely refused to venture downstairs into the basement.

I called in a friend of mine for help and he brought a small group of Buddhists who specialised in helping lost souls and haunting spirits. This was one of my first experiences of this work and I went to watch with interest. They chanted for about half an hour, rang bells and burnt incense before they started the rescue work.

I felt compelled to get involved and saw myself helping a number of men out of what seemed like a pit or cellar. They had to be helped out of the hole they were in. All was going well until one of the men refused my hand. I thought for a moment then put out both hands – this time he and another man each grabbed a hand and I pulled them out successfully this time. It would seem that they were friends or brothers, or maybe father and son, who refused to leave without each other.

We rescued twenty-two souls that night! We sensed that the men had been captives for some time before their deaths and had become conditioned with the mindset of captivity. Then they had been killed suddenly and violently, probably when a grenade or some other sort of bomb had been thrown into their prison.

The room was fine after they had moved on although it took some time to clear the effects of their long incarceration. The dogs stopped leaving their mark in the lounge, and whereas before they would never venture down the stairs they were now quite happy to visit the basement room.

Releasing a group from a school

Earlier I mentioned a psychic attack that I had once received in Singapore. On that visit I had been asked to clear a school. It was an unusual situation as the school had been bothered by a number of spirits for some considerable time and the previous year the school authorities had called in a local 'ghostbuster' – a terrible term but I'm afraid it sums up the attitude and style of this person's work. Some people see all spirits as a menace and vermin and treat them accordingly. This attitude really hurts me as I know that ghosts are just souls who have lost their way, in the same way as the living can sometimes lose their direction.

Anyway, this man had caught the spirits and pinned

them down in the school playing field. They hadn't caused the girls any further trouble but one of the teachers at the school was concerned that they were still there and asked me to release them – making sure, of course, that they didn't get back into the school.

I was a little apprehensive as the spirits had been quite rowdy and had frightened a lot of people in their time. However, the clearing was successful and I sent them on their way without any problems. I think their 'imprisonment' under the feet of hordes of teenage girls belting up and down the field playing hockey or whatever was enough to chasten them and they went to the light without any trouble at all!

Releasing souls under a curse

I once spent a day looking for a flat in London for my husband when a new job required him to be based in town during the week. I met up with a friend and we were led by a bright and enthusiastic young estate agent to the south side of the River Thames to look at a number of apartments that had been constructed in the old dockside and warehouses. These addresses had now become desirable as the old storehouses were being converted into residences after years of neglect.

The old warehouses had been used in the past for storing goods coming into London on trading ships. I didn't take to the area at all. I could feel the old stale energy of the years of neglect and decay. Even though the developers had done a great job of converting these tall and impressive buildings and the interiors were wonderful I didn't like the narrow and dark streets.

I could feel myself getting heavier and heavier as the young man kept up his non-stop line of bright chatter peppered with estate-agent-speak like 'no problem', 'desirable', 'fashionable', 'accessible' and so on.

As we were leaving and about to cross the river I felt a strong pull behind me. I opened up psychically and sensed a presence. I needed to stop to talk to it so I said to my friend 'keep him talking' while I pretended to have a problem with my shoe. 'What is it?' I asked. 'We need your help, we're stuck, can you let us go?' I said I would help but my new spirit acquaintance told me that there were many of them. I promised to return and help them all at some time in the future.

A month or so later we had moved into a flat on the other side of the river and I was visiting it with the Hearts and Hands' representative from Romania. We were doing a combination of workshop and London tour and planned to cover rescue work that day, so I decided it would be a good opportunity to help the group of spirits who had contacted me.

The experience we had was remarkable. As I started to work I was aware of a large number of people – I couldn't make out who they were but they were scruffy and dirty and dressed in the clothes of the Middle Ages. I immediately realised that a curse was involved. Then an angel – a really huge angel – came into my mind's eye and as I cleared the curse and the spirits were released, they flew off like corks out of a bottle, flying past me and straight to the light of the angel.

Other angels came flying in to help the many souls that had been affected – children, men and women. As they flew past me I could hear these fast-moving souls muttering something I couldn't catch so I stopped one and he said: 'God bless you, ma'am.'

The curse had been: 'May you rot in hell.' It seemed that these people were the first victims of the plague – I suspect they were the original sailors whose boat had brought the plague up the Thames, and their families. Obviously the good citizens of London were appalled at the threat they had brought to the city and cursed these innocents soundly. They were so terrified that they would indeed go to hell that their fear had kept them tied down ever since they had died. There may well have been others who had been castigated with this old curse as it was once commonly used in the past and hopefully they were all released that day.

Helping those who have just died

When you hear of someone who has died, send light and love to their soul. They will be well cared for on the other side but your love will help them to leave the Earth peacefully. Also if you see in the paper or on television that there has been a massacre or disaster with great loss of life then use the above process to help all those souls to pass on. If the disaster is reported in the newspaper then you can put your hand on the paper and also send love and healing using the healing symbol.

Living in Harmony with House Spirits

If you think you have a spirit in your home and you get the same response I did when I tried to help the young girl in Kuala Lumpur to the light, then you really have no other option than to learn to live with your spirit. All you have to do is ask him or her to please leave you alone and in peace. In return you can promise to let them stay without hassling them to leave. You will find that you can live in total harmony with a spirit as long as you respect it and look after the environment.

This reminds me of another situation that occurred in Malaysia. A friend and her husband had a lot of work to do on their new home so the Indonesian workers who were contracted to do the renovations moved in and used their house as temporary lodgings.

One night an apparition came to one of the workmen and declared that she was the spirit of the house and that she was very annoyed at the mess and generally untidy state of the place. She told the workman that if he and his colleagues would keep the house as tidy as possible while they stayed there she would reward them.

Once the poor man had recovered he told his companions and from that point they kept the place absolutely immaculate. On the last night of their stay the spirit reappeared and gave them a series of numbers for the national lottery – needless to say these were winning numbers! I was always aware of her presence in the house but despite making my bed dutifully whenever I stayed there, I didn't receive such good fortune – maybe I should have left the bathroom just a little tidier!

Visits from Angels and Divas

I have used the word 'soul' and 'spirit' interchangeably throughout this book. However, there are other forms of spirit that are not human souls. Many different types of being live in the etheric realms and many never appear in human form on Earth. This is a huge subject in itself but I briefly want to mention a few of these beings here as you may come into contact with them and I want you to be aware that there is a difference between the souls of humans who have not moved on and the angelic and divine presences that may come into your life.

Angels

How would you know if you are in the presence of an angel or a departed soul? The most significant difference is the vibrations that they emanate. A soul, especially one that is troubled in any way, will be fearful and therefore of low vibration and thus will make the atmosphere around it cool or cold. There will be an aspect of darkness associated with its presence, whereas an angel will bring light and uplift the surrounding atmosphere.

If you are lucky enough to meet an angel or see one with your inner sight – your mind's eye – then you will feel wonderful and blessed, and you will feel the great love that these glorious beings have for you.

Angels don't have free will as we do. We can choose whether we do the right or the wrong thing, but they are 'programmed' to do the right thing for everyone. Their whole essence is one of love, tolerance and compassion. They always work for your highest good. Angels will come when called and if you ask for their help at any time they will be with you, protecting and assisting you, although you may not see them.

Divas

Other spirits that you may come across are 'divas'. These are the spirits of nature. Every tree, plant, river, pond, rock and crystal will have its diva. Divas embody the blueprint, the spiritual essence, of the species of plant or rock and so on, and manifest themselves to us as the fairies of our childhood. When she was a child my mother had three fairies as companions, who were called Buttercup, Lampa and Ratta. She talked to them constantly up to the age of five and they were her dearest friends (I personally think her favourite was Ratta, who was the mischievous one, although even today I can't persuade her to tell me just what she and Ratta got up to!).

Someone I know told me of an incident that conclusively proved the existence of divas to her partner, who was somewhat sceptical. They arrived on a weekend break and settled into their accommodation, which was at the side of a lake.

Everything about the location was just perfect, apart from the accumulation of rubbish in the water, which spoiled the view and the harmony of their retreat. So she decided to ask the divas if they wouldn't mind cleaning up the area during the night. The next morning her partner was absolutely amazed and delighted to find that all the rubbish had disappeared between nightfall and dawn.

Bring in the Good Energies

We have now worked our way through all the forms of negative energy that can disturb our peace and finally arrived at the beautiful energies of the angels and divas that can bring love and light into our lives. Why do some people seem to attract negative situations and court misfortune in their lives and act as magnets for negative energies, while others sail through life as though encapsulated in a lucky bubble, attracting light and good fortune?

There are, of course, many reasons, but one is their attitude and what they expect from life. You may not be able to change everything in your world to gold but you can certainly take a positive stance on life. To draw towards you the positive things of life you need to be positive. With a positive attitude you can call in lighter and brighter aspects and people; with expectation and visualisation you can call good fortune into your life.

Finally, remember that you can always call in the angels. Just *intend* that you will receive help from the angelic realms and you will be surprised how quickly the angels will respond!

9

Choose the Positive

Let's conclude the book by looking at the way we can affect ourselves and our environment by our choice of the positive rather than the negative – by opting for high vibrations whether it be in our behaviour, thoughts and attitudes or in our food and drink. Being in balance is really important so let's try to avoid extremes and bring ourselves stability by taking a balanced approach to everything in our lives. This in turn will then affect the stability of our immediate group.

We will also look at accepting both the light and the dark within ourselves. The negativity around us will affect us far less if we see it through the bright light of our own happiness and positivity, so we will end with a statement of our commitment to our own personal happiness.

High and Low Vibrations – Some Guidelines

Some things only become harmful when you have them in excess. Alcohol is a good example. A glass or two of chilled white wine can be a wonderfully uplifting and enjoyable experience – your spirits will soar and you will become more relaxed. But consume a bottle or two and your resolve and control start to go and you will be open to the effects of any person and any energy that is around you, whether negative or positive. You are taken from a high vibration – an uplifted state – to a state of toxicity. Your body will start to feel dense and your organs will be working full-time to clear the negativity overload that you have created.

It's interesting that doctors are now suggesting that *moderate* drinking of alcohol can enhance our well-being. I know it. I also know that we each have our own understanding of moderation. I leave it to you to find out and intuit the point where you move from a positive state to a negative state when drinking. By the way, this is not something you can work out when you have a glass in your hand – intuition is one of the first faculties to leave you when intoxication sets in!

Personally I don't drink very much or very often but I do enjoy the odd glass to relax socially. For some of us one glass of wine or half a pint of beer or one gin and tonic is enough. I find that it depends on what I am doing, my state of mind and my food consumption.

Also you need to find out what type of drink suits you best. Just see how your body reacts. How do you feel emotionally? Your body's reactions and emotions are a wonderful barometer for checking all forms of negativity. Keep in touch with your feelings; listen to your senses rather than your brain. Your mind is capable of being programmed to tell you what you or others think you *should* know or do. But your true feelings come from within.

In the charts below I have listed examples of some of the things that give us high or low vibrations in various categories. These are guidelines and, of course, sometimes they will vary depending on your circumstances. For example, any food, no matter how mouldy and full of additives, will bring high vibrations to a starving person. If you use these guidelines with understanding and in the context of what I have said in this book I think you will get my message.

Drinks

Higher vibrations	**Lower vibrations**
Fresh mineral water	Water with high fluoride content
Spring water	Old static water
A couple of relaxing glasses of wine	Excess of alcohol
Caffeine-free herbal teas	Excess of coffee and tea
Freshly prepared fruit juices	Sugar-filled carbonated drinks

Food

Try always to choose natural, organic and fresh food, and eat it as unprocessed as possible. For example, a steak is better than a hamburger, wholemeal bread is better than white bread, and so on. Fresh food is better than tinned or even frozen. Try to avoid food with additives like artificial preservatives, colourings, chemicals, E-numbers and so on. But don't forget the old adage 'a little bit of what you fancy does you good' – in other words don't be too hard on yourself or puritanical!

Higher vibrations	**Lower vibrations**
Home-cooked (with positivity!)	Precooked and reheated
Honey	Refined sugar
Fructose	Artificial sweeteners
Wholemeal flour	Refined white flour
Free range or organic meat and eggs	Factory-farmed meat and eggs
Fresh vegetables	Tinned vegetables

At home

Higher vibrations	**Lower vibrations**
Fresh flowers and plants	Dead and dying, neglected plants
Bright, light-coloured decor and fabrics	Black or faded colours, dirty and soiled curtains and coverings
Tidy and clean	Cluttered and dirty
Lots of natural light	Dark and gloomy
Good source of fresh air and ventilation	Air conditioners, closed windows
Real fires	Imitation fires and central heating
Musical instruments	Non-stop use of computers
Conversation – light and positive	Arguments
Selective viewing of good TV programmes	Excessive and indiscriminate viewing, especially of violence

Board games	Excessive playing of video games
Any types of music – moderate levels	Long periods of loud, intrusive music of any kind

At the office

Higher vibrations	**Lower vibrations**
Happy, smiling, upbeat receptionist	'Dragon at the gate'
Fresh flowers and plants	Uncared for plants, dusty plastic imitations, or none at all
Supply of fresh, cool mineral water	Stewed coffee and tea from machines, urns or hotplates
Bright decor	Functional grey and bland decor
Rest room with homely environment	Excess of 'Don't' signs
Natural light	Fluorescent light
Openable windows for fresh air	Air conditioners and sealed windows
Open and constructive attitude	Negative gossip and backbiting
Encouragement to voice opinions	Oppressive and autocratic office culture
Informal, face-to-face contact between staff and managers	'Faceless bosses' communicating only through memos and e-mails
Teamwork	People working in isolation

Entertainment and relaxation

Higher vibrations	Lower vibrations
Circle of good friends	Excess of solitary pursuits
Laughter and fun	Excess of drink
Comfortable and intimate bars and clubs	Rough and rowdy places where people go to get 'off their faces' with alcohol and drugs
Light and bright places	Dark, gloomy and seedy places
Fresh-air activities, sports	Sitting indoors watching television on bright sunny days; being a 'couch potato'
Enjoying the skill and fun of a sports match	Hurling abuse at the opposing team
Reading uplifting, informative or exciting books and articles	Reading about violence or pornography
Concerts of all kinds	Taking drugs of any kind
Meditation	Long lie-ins and frequent dozing on the sofa
Plenty of good sleep	Sleep deprivation or insomnia

Keeping an Emotional Balance

As you will see from the above lists, which I repeat are guidelines only, most situations are a problem only when they become excessive. They harm us when they get out of hand, out of control. Our emotions can be seen in the same way. Often a feeling, attitude or emotional response can be wonderfully positive and helpful to ourselves and others when it is at one end of the spectrum – but can become harmful and disruptive to all around when it swings too far the other way. This means that really and truthfully there is no such thing as a bad emotion – just that too much of one emotion or another can be a problem. Let's look at some examples.

Passion

This can be a wonderful feeling. It makes us move, it allows us to enjoy life to the fullest. It's the passion we feel for art, music, literature and so on that makes us uplifted. It's our passion for beliefs and rights and spiritual truths that makes us change the world.

Passionate people are full of life, they are strong-willed, they are dynamic. They have zeal and express what they feel. In other words, this is a great emotion. But if we take it too far, passion becomes anger and aggression. This creates problems for ourselves and for everyone who shares our lives.

Calm

Calm is the perfect state. It's what we are all looking for and if we are a calm, peaceful and laid-back person we spread this to everyone around us. Wonderful, but if we get too laid-back we can move into the realms of not bothering about anything and anyone, not reacting, not caring. This in turn can go as far as self-indulgence and selfishness.

Loving

We all want to be in the state of love, unconditionally loving and accepting everyone, including ourselves, exactly as they are, just perfect. However, love can easily turn into over-protectiveness. This will stop people from growing naturally. It can become conditional and manipulative – 'I will love you if . . .'. It can become smothering. It can become possessiveness.

Accepting the Dark and Light in Yourself

We all have negativity inside us. Everyone has what is often called a 'shadow side'. Of course we do. We need to recognise this aspect of ourselves and then embrace it and love it too. Most unhappiness comes from within, from a lack of self-acceptance – a lack of love and respect for ourselves. We see the darkness within us and we reject it. We think 'I am so selfish/thoughtless/angry/jealous' and so on. Then we dislike ourselves. This is compounded by negative experiences and by the things that are said to us, especially in childhood, and especially by our parents.

Be happy with yourself

We all make mistakes, we all hurt people sometimes, we have all done things 'wrong', we have all failed at something. To become happy we need to be happy with ourselves, but as long we focus on and then reject the dark side of ourselves – the things we list as 'wrong with us' – then we cannot be happy. Happiness is an internal state, not something to find outside. Inner happiness comes from accepting both sides of our nature, the light and the dark.

Write down all the things that you don't like about yourself. Then say to yourself: 'But never mind, I'm still me, I am trying to get better, I am learning from my mistakes, I accept me as I am.' Remember, the only reason you are on this Earth is because you need to find inner happiness, which in turn leads to enlightenment – the most spiritual and uplifting experience of our evolution.

If you were already perfect in every way, had learnt all the lessons, been there, done it – you would be sitting on your cloud with your harp now and laughing at all us mortals struggling to get it right! Believe in yourself, let go of your guilt and learn to get on with yourself – make yourself your best friend.

A Final Affirmation – Commit to Your Own Happiness

To end this book on managing the negative energies we will encounter in life, I offer you this affirmation to meditate on. I suggest you say it out loud:

> *I accept all aspects of myself and through this I acknowledge myself in totality. I see myself as a unique and special person who deserves happiness. I will not continually castigate myself for what I haven't done but congratulate myself for what I have achieved. I know that as I work at being happier within myself so I make those around me happier too.*
>
> *I realise that happiness is not an item to be bought, won, given, taken or acquired but something I can create*

for myself, within myself. I no longer need the darker and low vibrations of life to give me fulfilment and pleasure. I choose my pleasures from the highest vibrations and from that which uplifts my life. I draw towards me all those things and people that make me feel good about myself. I commit to associating with the very highest vibrations of energy of light and love.

I attract people who are passionate but not angry, calm but not selfish, loving but not possessive. These people will share my life and we will have mutually beneficial relationships. I commit to creating true happiness and as I create it, so I will keep it.

Postscript

Why do we have evil in the world?
To enable us to value light.

We need darkness to allow us to see
and to appreciate the light.

There is darkness in our world to let us value the light, unpleasantness to let us value decency and cruelty to let us value kindness. But remember just to look, observe, evaluate then move on – don't spend too long with the darkness. Don't allow yourself to become entranced by it. Don't allow yourself to be fearful of its powers. Look at evil – see the message that it has for you then move off and step into the light. Take the positive track – it is the best way home and it is well lit.

Create your own personal light source
with your positive attitude!

Further Reading

Books

J. Barnard, *A Guide to the Bach Flower Remedies*, C.W. Daniel, 1979

Dr F. Batmanghelidj, *Your Body's Many Cries for Water*, Tagman Press, 2000

Susan Curtis, Romy Fraser and Irene Kohler, *Neal's Yard Natural Remedies*, Penguin Arkana, 1988

John Edward, *One Last Time*, Piatkus, 1998. A psychic medium speaks to those we have loved and lost.

Richard P. Feynman, *Six Easy Pieces: The Fundamentals of Physics Explained by Its Most Brilliant Teacher*, Penguin Books, 1963. An accessible guide to physics based on undergraduate lectures given by this Nobel-Prize-winning American scientist (1918–1988).

Judy Hall, *The Illustrated Guide to Crystals*, Godsfield Press, 2000

Soozi Holbeche, *The Power of Crystals*, Piatkus, 1990

Patrick Holford, *The Optimum Nutrition Bible*, Piatkus, 1997

Karen Kingston, *Creating Sacred Space with Feng Shui*, Piatkus, 1996

Andreas Moritz, *The Amazing Liver Cleanse*, St Anne's Press, 1988

Michael Newton, *Journey of Souls: Case Studies of Life Between Lives*, Llewellyn Publications, 1994

Michael Newton, *Destiny of Souls: New Case Studies of Life between Lives*, Llewellyn Publications, 2001

Ron and Ann Procter, *Healing Sick Houses*, Gateway, Dublin, 2000

Elizabeth Clare Prophet, *The Violet Flame*, Summit University Press, 1997

Readers Digest Association, *Foods that Harm, Foods that Heal*, 1996

James Redfield, *The Celestine Prophecy*, Bantam Books, 1994

Keith Scott-Mumby, *Virtual Medicine*, Thorsons, 1999

Jane Scrivner, *Detox Yourself*, Piatkus, 1998

Jane Scrivner, *Total Detox – 6 Ways to Revitalise Your Life*, Piatkus, 2000

Lillian Too, *The Fundamentals of Feng Shui*, Element, 2000

Vladislav Vaclavek, *Magnotherapy – the Phacts*, Cobett & Cavanagh, 1999

Victor Vermeulen and Jonathan Ancer, *The Victor Within*, Tenacity Publications, 2000. PO Box 92043, Norwood, 2117, South Africa. Tel.: 011 640 6722. Inspirational book on the ability of a young man to overcome the limitations and depression of the accident that made him a quadriplegic. For copies of the book contact June Cassie on +2711 640 6722. To book Victor for talks contact Leigh Sinclair on +2711 793 5330.

Richard Webster, *Dowsing for Beginners*, Llewellyn Publications, 1996

Dr Brian Weiss, *Many Lives, Many Masters*, Piatkus, 1994

Stuart Wilde, *Affirmations*, Hay House, 1987

Magazines

Electromagnetic Hazard and Therapy. A quarterly news report on all aspects of this subject sent to subscribers. Tel.: (01273) 452744. Website: www.perspective.co.uk

Outrage. The magazine of Animal Aid, the Old Chapel, Bradford St, Tonbridge, Kent TN9 1AW, United Kingdom. Tel.: (01732) 364546.

Viva (*Vegetarians International Voice for Animals*). 12 Queen Square, Brighton, East Sussex BN1 3FD, United Kingdom. Tel.: (01273) 777688. Website: www.viva.org.uk

Other organisations and websites

CIWF (Compassion in World Farming). This organisation does wonderful work lobbying governments to prevent cruelty to farm animals on farms and in transportation. Contact: CIWF, 5a Charles Street, Petersfield, Hampshire GU32 3EH, United Kingdom. Tel.: (01730) 264208. E-mail: compassion@ciwf.co.uk. Website: www.ciwf.co.uk

For another perspective on mobile phones: www.grn.es/electropolicies/cellplague.htm

For an excellent list of complementary and alternative therapies: www.whatmedicine.co.uk

Hearts and Hands

Healing with Love and Compassion

Hearts and Hands is a non-profit-making organisation that is dedicated to spreading the understanding of natural healing throughout the world. We have trained facilitators and healers throughout the world who can lead, guide, teach and support you. For further information on our workshops and meditation meetings please contact us at Hearts and Hands Healing in the UK: 21 Honey Lane, Burley, Ringwood, Hampshire BH24 4EN, or visit our website www.heartshands.org, or email us at care@heartshands.org

Hearts and Hands has representatives and teachers in the following countries: UK, USA, Malaysia, Romania, Singapore, Hong Kong, Russia, South Africa and Australia. Please contact Hearts and Hands in the UK for names and contact numbers.

The following are also available from Hearts and Hands:

- Guided meditation CDs with Anne Jones.
- Natural room sprays for clearing buildings and personal auras.
- Aromatherapy oils – healing blends.
- Crystal sets for chakra balancing and energising.

Please email us to receive regular updates on our workshops and seminars for self-healing and energy healing. Visit our website to request distant healing from our network of healers for yourself, family and friends.

Index

Please note: page numbers in *italics* refer to diagrams.

active negativity 162–4
acupressure 76
acupuncture 76
addiction 52–4, 60–2
adrenaline junkies 49–50
aegirine 241
affirmations 68, 279–80
Africa 226, 227
air pollution 192–5
alcohol consumption 272–3
allergies, food 137, 138, 144–5
amethyst 122
amulets 115–17, 241
angels 241–2, 260–2, 265, 267–8, 270
anger 99–101
animals 214
Anti-Smoking for Health (ASH) 61
antiques 155–6
apache tears 124–5
apophyllite crystal tips 188
aromatherapy oils 74, 119–20, 166
art 156–7, 178
astral plane 18
auras 35–43, *36*
  clearing 43, 59–60, 127–30
  colour 38
  combing 60
  defining 35
  layers 37
  lightening 42–3
  protecting 40
  shape 40–2
  sweeping 43, 59–60
  and thought forms 45
  and vibrations 39–40
aversion therapy 62

Bach Flower Remedies 75, 104
'bad luck syndrome' 203

bagua 179–80, *179*
base chakra 123
bathrooms 177
baths 118
beams 178
bedrooms 176–7
bells 167
bereavement 54–5
Bernadette 88
black magic 225–34
  defining 226–7
  lifting 19–21, 23–4, 228–33
  protection from 233–4
  types 227–8
  witches 225–6
black tourmaline 123
blessings
  for food 140–1
  for places 169–71
  for protection against psychic attack 241
blocks (energy) 45–6, 60
blue lace agate 122
bomos 20, 21
books, energy of 176–7
boundaries, personal 126–30
bovine spongiform encephalopathy (BSE) 135
bubble, the (protective technique) 114
building materials 158–9
buildings
  see also houses
  energy of 157–72, 203–4

calmness 277
calories 132, 142
carbohydrates 148–9
Carnarvon, Lord 15–16
carnelian 123
Carter, Howard 15–16, 17
cats 214
causality 221, 235–6
cedarwood oil 119
chakras
  balancing with crystals 120–4
  balancing with symbols 126
  types *121*, 122–3
chanting 166–7
children
  abuse of 55
  angry 100
  spirits of 254–5
chiropractic 77
Christianity 88, 224–5, 231
Churchill, Winston 93
cities 162–3
citrine 123
clapping 167–8
cleaning up/clear outs 164, 172–4
cleansing negative energy 117–26, 157
  from auras 43, 59–60, 127–30
  from buildings 164–72
  from purchases 157
clock radios 190–1
clothing 73, 173
Coenzyme Q10 79
colonic irrigation 147–8
colour therapy 72–3
computers 188–9, 197
conditioning, of negative attitudes 50–2
cooking 139–40, 141
Cotswolds 160–1
Creuzfeldt-Jakob disease (vCJD) 135

crown chakra 122
crystal bowls 32–3, 167
crystal drops 178
crystals
for chakra balancing 120–4
to absorb electromagnetic energy 188–9
for letting go of problems 124–5
protective 115–17, 241, 242
recharging/cleansing 115–16
culture 50–2
curses 220–2, 225
lifting 19–21, 23–4, 228–31
protection from 239–44
recognizing 236–9
on spirits 264–6
cymbals 167

dairy products 138
dance 78–9
death 245–8, 249–50
defining energy 33–5
depression 47
detox
for the body 145–7
for the home 172–4
Diana, Princess of Wales 90–1
distance healing 14, 44
helping spirits to move on 19
overcoming self-negativity 65–7
for the planet 218–19
symbol for 65–7, *65*
dithering 110–11
divas 267, 268–9
divining rods 205–8, *206*–7
dogs 214
dominance 92–3
dowsing 28, 204–13
at a distance 210–13
with divining rods 205–8, *206*–7
with pendulums 205, 209–13
drinks 79, 147–8, 194, 272–3

Earth, healing meditation for 218–19
Earth energies 25–9, 184, 185, 198–219
Earth energy lines 25–8, 198–202
detection 204–14
negative 200–2, 214–17, 252
eating out 139–40
echinacea 79–80
egg, the (protective technique) 113–14
egotism 106
Egypt 14–19
electric power points 190
electromagnetic stress 26–7, 185–98
air pollution 192–5
individual susceptibility to 195
sources 187–91
electromagnetic therapy 74
emotions
balancing 276–8
negative 54–8
over-emotional people 102–4
enemas 147

energy boosters 69–80, 148–9
energy checks 98
energy drains 104–5
energy flow 174–83
energy healing 72
energy imprints 2, 21–4
energy links 22–4
energy showers 42–3
enlightenment 246–7, 279
entertainment 80, 276
entrance halls 176
etheric corridors 256
eucalyptus oil 119
exercises
  attracting positivity 63–4, 71–2
  aura cleansing 127–30
  blessing houses 170–1
  chakra balancing 123–4
  clearing curses/spells 241–4
  distance healing 66–7
  dowsing for Earth energies 208, 209–10, 211–12
  Earth energy healing 215–16
  energy checks 98
  Feng Shui 179–80
  for filling the self with light 81–3
  giving up smoking 62
  healing food 141
  helping souls to the light 261–2
  letting go of problems 124
  for lightening auras 42–3
  planetary healing meditation 218–19
  releasing negative energy 125–6
  self-protective 117
  space clearing 169

families 50–2, 54–5, 96–8
fanaticism 94
farming conditions 134–6, 138, 139
fearfulness 108–9, 135–6
Feng Shui 174–83
Feng Shui grids (*bagua*) 179–80, *179*
Feynman, Richard P. 34–5, 44
fish 136–7, 149
flower remedies 74–5, 104
flowers 178
fluorescent lighting 190
flying 86
focus 41
food 79, 131–49, 273–4
four trees (protective technique) 240
front doors 175–6
fruit 148
furniture 155–6

gallbladder, stones 145, 146
garage door, the (protective technique) 114
Geldof, Bob 93
gemstone therapy 73
geopathic stress 25–9, 184, 185, 198–219, 252
ghosts *see* spirits
ginseng 79
golden pyramid, the (protective technique) 114–15
golden trees (protective technique) 240
gossip 95
grief 54–5

group energy
effect of 85–7
negative 90–1, 92–6
thought forms 87–96

Haiti 231
handicrafts 156–7
happiness 279–80
harmony symbol 171, *171*
hate 231–3
headaches 46, 60
healing 12–13, 30
of curses/black magic 19–21
distance healing 14, 44, 65–7, *65*, 218–19
energy healing 72
food 141–2
and magic 222–3
of negative Earth energies 214–17
symbols for 65–7, *65*, 71–2, *71*, 168–9, *169*, 171, 216, 218–19, 243
and witchcraft 224–5
healing space 80–1
health
effects of electromagnetic stress 186
effects of life stresses 47–8
and thought forms 46
heart chakra 122–3
Hearts and Hands organisation 14, 32, 72, 91–2, 265
heaven 247
hell 247–8
herbal teas 79
Hitler, Adolf 93, 227–8
houses
decorating 11–12
detoxing 172–4
effects of negative Earth energies 203–4
healing negative Earth energies 214–17
energy levels of 27–9
Feng Shui tips for 174–83
vibrations of 274–5
hypnotherapy 246–7

immunity, low 47
inactive negativity 162
incense 165
individual energy 92–3, 96–8
Indonesia 94
intuition 126–7
ionisers 194–5
ions, negative 192–5
Iraq 22–3

Japan 88–90
Jesus Christ 88
jewellery 151–5
juniper oil 119

kidneys
detoxing 147
stones 145, 146
Kirlian photography 38
Kuala Lumpur 32, 205, 254–5, 262–3

landscapes, energy of 159–62
laughter 80
lethargy 27–9, 46
ley lines 25–8, 199–200, 202, 214
life experience 54–9
lighting, fluorescent 190
lime oil 119

liver
  detoxing 147
  stones 145, 146
Lourdes 88
love
  attracting 236
  for the self 52, 278–9
  smothering 97, 109–10

mad cow's disease 135
magic 220, 222–44
  black 19–21, 23–4, 225–34
  modern 234–6
  recognizing psychic attacks 236–9
Malaysia 10–12, 14–15, 19–20, 32, 140, 175, 205, 213, 226, 254–5, 262–3, 267
mantras 166–7
Mary (mother of Jesus) 88
mass suicide 93
massage 76
mealtimes 143
meat 133–6
medication 144
meditation
  for filling the self with light 81–3
  for lightening auras 42
  for planetary healing 218–19
memorials 183–4
meridians *36*, 37–8, 45
'Michael and Mary' line 199
microwaves 191
mindsets 50–1
miracles 88
mobile phones 189–90
mobs 93–5
Moon 217–18
Moritz, Andreas 146–7
Morris, William 173
motivation 61, 62
music 78, 166
Muslims 233

nations 88–90
Native American tradition 92, 118–19, 124, 165
nature 70, 193–4
'negative energy magnets' 269
Newton, Michael 246
night attacks 237–8
no, learning to say 127
nutritional supplements 79–80

objects, energy of 150–7
obsidian 188
offices 95–6, 275
oils, aromatherapy 74, 119–20, 166
orange oil 119
organic farming 136, 138, 139
orthodox medicine 37
other people's negativity 24, 85–130
Ouija 256–60
over-emotional people 102–4
over-zealousness 112–13
oxygen depletion 192, 193–4

partners, attracting 236
passion 277
passive negativity 85–6
past-life regression 246–7
patterns/habits, negative 52
pendulums, for dowsing 205, 209–13

personal boundaries 126–30
personality traits, difficult 99–113
perspective 67
physical disablement 56–7
physical exercise 194
physics 33–5
places
  see also buildings; houses
  energy of 157–64, 183–4
planetary healing meditation 218–19
plants 177–8
poltergeists 252–4
portals 256
Portsmouth 161–2
positive energy
  choosing 269–70, 271–80
  connecting to 69–72
  group 88, 91–3
positive people 69
positive thought
  affirmations 68, 279–80
  generating 30
  power of 44, 63–8
  turning negative thoughts into 58–62
poultry 133–4
prayer 65
problems, letting go of 124
Proctor, Anne 190
Proctor, Roy 190
protection
  for auras 40
  from group energies 86–7
  from magic 233–4
  from negative energy 113–17
  from psychic attacks 239–44
  symbol for 239, *240*, 243
psychic attacks
  protection 239–44
  recognizing 236–9
psychometry 152

quartz
  clear 117, 122, 167, 188, 215–16
  rose 122–3

rape 55–6
ready-made meals 139–40
Red Tide 137
reflexology 76–7
Reiki 170, 234
relaxation 48–50, 276
release symbol 125–6, *125*, 168, *168*, 243
room sprays, natural 165, 215, 216
running water (protective technique) 240–1

sacral chakra 123
sage 118–19, 165
salt 118, 168
sandalwood 120, 165
seasonal affective disorder (SAD) 29
'seeing' 13–14
self-acceptance 278–80
self-appraisal
  negative 50–2
  positive 58
self-esteem 50–3, 107–8
self-love 52, 278–9
self-negativity, overcoming 31–84
self-pity 104–5
self-respect 127
sensing negative energy 31–3

sensitive people, protection for 40
September 11th, 2001 94, 233
'shadow side' 278–9
shamans 20
shellfish 137
Shiatsu 76
'sick building syndrome' 204
silver cloak, the (protective technique) 115
Singapore 228–30
singing bowls 167
smoking, giving up 61–2
smudging 118–19, 157, 165
society 50–2
solar plexus chakra 123
sorrow, group 90–1
Spion Kop, South Africa 159
spirit guides 13, 241, 246
spirits 1–2, 8–10, 11, 245–70
  attraction to geopathic stress 202, 252
  curses on 264–6
  hell 248
  helping them to move on 10, 14–19, 28, 244, 253, 260–6
  helping those who have just died 266
  living in harmony with house spirits 266–7
  reasons for staying earth-bound 249–52
  'seeing' 14
  witnessing apparitions 249
sport 77–8
spring cleaning 172–4
stabilising symbol 243, *243*
static electricity 192–3
stones, gallbladder/kidney/liver 145, 146
stress 47–50
stubbornness 101–2
suicide, mass 93
sulking 105–6
swastikas 227–8
symbols
  distance healing 65–7, *65*
  harmonious 171, *171*
  healing 65–7, *65*, 71–2, *71*, 168–9, *169*, 171, 216, 218–19, 243
  protective 239, *240*, 243
  for releasing negative energy 125–6, *125*, 168, *168*, 243
  stabilising 243, *243*

tearfulness 102–4
teenagers 99, 100
televisions 188
terminators 215
Third Eye chakra 122
thought
  effects of 44–5
  as energy 43–5
  negative 29–30, 44–5, 58–62
  positive 30, 44, 58–68, 279–80
thought forms 45–7, 58
  in addiction 53–4
  getting rid of negative 59–60
  group 87–96
throat chakra 122
toilets 177
tourmaline 188
travel 86
Turkey 21–3

Tutankhamun 15–18

universal energies,
  connecting to 70–2, *71*, 72
unreliability 111–12

Valley of the Artisans 18–19
Valley of the Kings 15–18
vegans 133
vegetables 138–9, 148
Vermeulen, Victor 56–7
vibrations 43
  and auras 39–40
  of food 141–2
  receiving high/avoiding low 272–6
  sending out positive 65
Video Operator's Distress Syndrome (VODS) 193
visualisation 62
  for aura cleansing 127–30
  for filling the self with light 81–3
  power of 63–4
  protective 113–15
Voodoo 231

water
  consumption 147–8, 194
  as energy carrier 202
  running 120
water features 178
Weiss, Brian 247
wind chimes 178
witchdoctors 23–4, 226, 227
witches 25, 224–6
writers block 45–6

yoga 78

Also by Anne Jones

Heal Yourself, also published by Piatkus Books, was Anne Jones's first book. It is an all-round, practical guide to healing your body, mind, emotions and soul through the power of positive thinking.

£10.99 ISBN 0 7499 2295 8